# No One
# Had More
# FUN

# No One
# Had More
# FUN

## JOE McKASTY

*Legwork Team Publishing*
*New York*

Legwork Team Publishing
New York
www.legworkteam.com

Second Edition 10/14/2015
First Edition 08/31/2015

Printed in the United States of America
This book is printed on acid-free paper
Designed by Vaiva Ulenas-Boertje

I wish to dedicate this book
to my beloved wife, Georgia,
who left her lasting memory on all
who were touched by her irreplaceable
personality, and to those readers
meeting her for the first time within
the pages of this loving memoir.

### *Ein Prosit*

Ein Prosit, Ein Prosit
Der Gemutlichkeit
Ein Prosit, Ein Prosit
Der Gemutlichkeit
Eins! Zwei! Drei! G'Suffa!
Zicke, Zacke,—Zicke, Zacke,
Hoi, Hoi, Hoi.

A Toast, A Toast
To cheer and good times
A Toast, A Toast
To cheer and good times.

# CONTENTS

# CONTENTS

# PREFACE

The death of a beloved spouse is tragic and heart-breaking. Remembering and writing about the good times helps ease the pain as I pay tribute to Georgia's legacy. She dramatically touched the lives of people, many who were longtime friends, and also some newly introduced friends, which verified her legacy as a people person. She enjoyed maintaining those long term friendships and developing new ones. She had quite a few best friends and no one was a stranger in her house.

This book was written to share the memories of the many, many, good and fun times we had together, the places we traveled to, and the people who partook in those activities with us. Georgia enjoyed entertaining old friends, meeting new ones, and going to events, celebrations, and parties. Any gathering was reason enough to join the festivities and have some fun.

Some people consider themselves lucky if they travel to a foreign destination once or twice in their lifetime. Georgia has been fortunate enough to have done so many trips during her life. All the ones I have

# PREFACE

accompanied her on were fantastic journeys where each could be considered a vacation of a lifetime. She enjoyed life to the fullest, making the best out of any and every situation.

She was proud of her Greek-Irish heritage, was devoted to her family, and truly loved her neighbors, friends, and most of the people she came in contact with. I want to share those journeys, gatherings, parties, and all the fun times we had. I want to show the effect she had on other people and present their memories of her. I also share the pain I felt and the grief I went through during the difficult times at the end. Recounting all of this and dwelling on the good times has lessened the pain, and I really don't know of anyone who has had more fun.

# ACKNOWLEDGMENTS

I want to thank all who helped me throughout this difficult time and especially those who contributed their written feelings about Georgia.

Thank you Lisa for the early editing, Zac and John at Sea Haven for the Greek spelling, Rob and Jess from Berger Brothers Camera & Video, and Jane, Carol, and Stephen for your testimonials.

I especially want to thank everyone who allowed us to photograph them sharing our special moments of fun. These photos are an integral part of memories shared in this book.

I acknowledge the dedicated efforts of Janet Yudewitz, Russell Sacco and Vaiva Ulenas-Boertje of Legwork Team Publishing. I extend my gratitude to the team of design, editorial, and technical professionals for assisting me in transforming my attempt to immortalize Georgia into the book you now hold in your hands.

# ACKNOWLEDGMENTS

We have both been very fortunate to have met so many wonderful people in our journey together, at home in our daily lives, and in our worldly travels.

# Getting To Know Her

**D**amn it! She was right. It's not that I wasn't listening to what she was saying; it was that I didn't want to hear what she was saying. Thinking back now on the last few years, the signs were there.

One of the first was her inability to make the sometimes long trek to our airport gate when we were flying somewhere, or to hustle to another gate on connecting flights. Because of this, she had to have wheelchair service the last few years. But it got us to the gates on time, and we proceeded to have fun wherever our destination was. That's what being with Georgia was all about; no one has had more fun in their life than she has had. She was about meeting people, having parties, going places, and doing things. She made an impression on a lot of the people she met and had the gift of making long term friends with many of them.

Our relationship started when I organized a "Thirty-Year Dropout Reunion." I called it that because, having dropped out of high school on my sixteenth birthday, I wasn't in any yearbooks and I never got invited to high school class reunions. I did get my GED diploma while in the service, an Associate of Arts Degree thirteen years later, and a Bachelor of Science Degree the year I retired, but I still enjoy organizing and having those Dropout Reunions. They are fun because, besides dropouts, graduates from various years and friends from other towns attended also. At that particular one, we had gifts for various categories, such as a Thirty-Year Dropout Reunion souvenir tee-shirt for the person who had traveled the farthest and a McDonald's gift certificate for the person who had gained the most weight. But I wanted to get a nice gift for the couple who had been married the longest.

I decided on a gift certificate to Georgia's German Restaurant. It was a local place and a former hangout of some of the people coming to the reunion, when it had been called Onkel Herman's, and after that, Moose's Place. Georgia bought it in 1979. It had been a local clam digger, construction worker, pool-playing bar under Onkel, and a topless joint under Moose. She turned it into an excellent, inexpensive, and popular German restaurant—a smart move in a German town for a Greek-Irish girl who was born and raised in Manhattan. In later years, she catered one of those Dropout Reunions.

I went to the restaurant to get the certificate the night before our reunion and Georgia was there. We knew each other, but it was a vague relationship, having seen each other four or five times before. When Georgia had to do some banking business in town, she would park in the lot behind the Village Pub which was a few doors down from the bank. Millie, my girlfriend (I considered it a common-law marriage) owned it at that time. Millie and Georgia got along very well because Millie had four daughters; two of them were named Georgia and Kelly. Georgia's sister was named Calliope, but was called Calli or Kelly. Seagram's VO was Millie's and Georgia's mother, Eleanor's drink of choice. Once in a while when Ellie needed an outing and Georgia needed a break, she would drop Ellie off at Millie's Village Pub and have Millie call her when it was time to have someone pick her up. So there was a stronger bond or relationship between Georgia and Millie than there was between Georgia and me, as I only saw Georgia on a few of those occasions. Unfortunately, Millie died in 1983 and this was 1986.

## FIRST DATE

Georgia and I got to talking. She knew I had the summers off and asked if I had ever gone on a cruise. I told her no, that I hadn't, but it was on my list to do so one day. She asked if I would be interested in going on a cruise to Bermuda. As soon as I told her "yes," she went right to the phone, called her travel agent, got prices and dates for a one week cruise for the two of us departing in two weeks, and asked if I would be interested. Again I replied in the affirmative, but told her I would have to come back on Monday to pay for my share of the cost, which I did. We arranged for her bartender, Stephen, to drive us to the ship on Saturday morning and I did not see or talk to her until then, other than to call her Friday night to confirm the rendezvous time. I found out later that Stephen had asked her if she could trust this man she barely knew—to spend one week in the same room (and bed) with him. She said she could, and she did.

We agreed to an arrangement. If she got lucky and wanted to spend some time alone with someone else in our room, I would take a walk around the ship and spend some time in one of the lounges. If I got lucky, she would take the walk and hang out in the lounge. The first two nights, neither one of us got lucky. On the third night, we both got lucky when she seduced me. It was the beginning of our adventure.

When we got to Bermuda, it was also clear that she had another purpose in mind for me. She used me for declaring German beer steins when we went through customs. There is a limit on the amount you can declare as an individual. I don't remember the exact amount back then, but I think it was about $500 per person. She bought more than the two of us could claim, so she asked another couple we had just met, Frank and Patty on their honeymoon, if they would claim some steins for her. They agreed to do it and we rode to their place in New Jersey a few weeks later to pick up those steins as we traveled to Mercer, Pennsylvania in our motor home to see Georgia's Aunt Mary and Uncle John. She formed another one of her many lifelong relationships with Frank and Patty and has been in touch with them and their two daughters all these years since, sending the girls Christmas gifts every year.

While at a popular tourist bar on Front Street in Bermuda, a bartender named Princely, I believe, made us a fancy rum cocktail guaranteed to make us fall in love because we told him this was our first date. We had a few of those cocktails and I guess they worked because everything was a blur for a long time after that cruise.

*Princely*

## ANOTHER BERMUDA TRIP

On another one of our Bermuda trips, our flight was cancelled and there was a mad scramble to reschedule another flight to get there. As we waited on long lines, we befriended two Bermudians—Lynn, a local fisherman and his wife who was an elementary school principal. Because of Georgia's charm, we were invited to their home one day while we were vacationing there. His wife planned to take Georgia shopping at a local mart while Lynn invited me to accompany him and his crew of two mates to go out on his boat to haul fish traps.

Georgia is not a shopper and had a stronger interest in fishing than I did. She declined Lynn's wife's offer to go shopping and requested to go out on the boat with the boys. Lynn explained that there was no bathroom, and there may be rough seas causing conditions that could be unsuitable. But that did not deter Georgia. She had been in rough seas before and she could be out on a boat all day long and not have to go to the bathroom once. The weather was perfect with clear blue skies. The calm waters of Bermuda were a beautiful turquoise, and the fish were plentiful. I recorded this adventurous episode in our lives on video as we watched the mates haul in those traps which were about five by five by two feet. While boating to the next trap, the two mates became "filleting machines" as they filled buckets with fillets of the various brightly colored fish pulled from the previous trap. Occasionally, sharks would surround the boat to feast on the carcasses thrown overboard.

Lynn said he had had a dream the night before, that he would catch seven rockfish which I believe are equivalent to our jewfish. Toward the end of the day in one of the last traps was a huge rockfish—number seven. It was the only fish in the trap because it had eaten all the other fish. Lynn declared we would eat that fish that same night in the restaurant on Front Street in the heart of town where Georgia and I had had the drink guaranteed to make us fall in love. On video, we have his crew carrying that fish into the restaurant, which we did dine on later with Lynn and his wife. You can't get a more freshly served dinner than that. And it all started because she befriended some strangers while standing in line.

And later, on another Bermuda trip, Georgia and I volunteered to bring my best friend Sonny, and his wife Carol, to the airport for their 25th wedding anniversary excursion to Bermuda. We didn't tell them we also booked that same flight and as I unloaded the luggage, he asked, "What's with all this extra baggage?" It was then that I told him we were going there, also. We hooked up with our Bermudian friends, played golf, dined out, and really enjoyed a beautiful week. And it was all because Georgia suggested we join Sonny and Carol in their anniversary celebration.

I moved in with her shortly after that first Bermuda trip, and I can tell you, nobody has had more fun in their lifetime than Georgia. We went on many more cruises and vacations after that first one, including

*Sonny, Carol, Lynn, his wife, Georgia, and I*

*Georgia parasailing*

trips to the Eastern and Western Caribbean, Alaska, Bermuda several more times, Hawaii, Germany, Costa Rica, the Florida Keys, Las Vegas, and many trips in our motor home.

## MORTGAGE BURNING PARTY

During those early courtship years, I went with Georgia on my first trip to Germany. She wanted to make her last payment on a ten year note to Onkel Herman in Germany in Deutsche Marks. She made it a mortgage-burning party and arranged to have Eric, a friend of hers, pick up the Deutsche Marks. He was a friend she bought her house from in Amityville when he decided to move back to Germany. On video, we have Georgia presenting Onkel with his last payment as she dumped a bag full of Deutsche Marks on the table in front of him. He said, "It looks a little short." She replied, "It doesn't matter because you're going to be spending it all on us this week, anyway." Well, there was another week of partying as we helped Onkel spend his last payment. We had to encourage him to leave bigger tips for the servers because he was reluctant to keep spending his money and he was very frugal when leaving tips.

It was fun to be in Germany. The people are genuinely appreciative of tourists and all the restaurants pride themselves on serving the best beer and food. With Germany's purity laws banning artificial ingredients, they all did serve the best as we covered a good portion of Germany tasting great beer and good wines. On our last day there, Georgia went to reimburse Eric for the Deutsche Marks he had picked up for her to pay Onkel. He said she had given him too much. Instead of getting a thousand U. S. dollars converted to Deutsche Marks, he had only gotten one thousand Deutsche Marks when the exchange was about three to one. So Onkel was right; the pile was a little short. When we got back to the States though, Georgia had another mortgage-burning party at the restaurant and gave Onkel a check for the full amount of that last payment which he spent in Germany. He said he wouldn't have been so reluctant to spend the original "last payment" if he had known he was going to get another one.

Georgia loved Onkel Herman. By selling her his place, he helped her gain independence and she became a part of his family. Linus and Carol, two of Onk's children are like brother and sister to her. Thirty-five years later, we were invited to Carol's two son's weddings—one last year with Chester and Jessica in Lake George, and one this year with Casey and Sydney in Alabama. Georgia has been involved in many of Onk's family affairs and gatherings. Thanks to him she was able to prove herself and ran a successful business. Georgia's German Restaurant was her baby and she was proud of it.

When she took the place over from him, she turned it from a local bar into a popular restaurant with lunch specials, inexpensive dinners, and good German food, specializing in sauerbraten and wursts. One of her slogans was, "We serve the best of the wurst." Naturally, she had German beer on tap and held many Jägermeister parties. She had many Oktoberfest events on the premises and built up a reputation and a following. Everyone knew if you went to Georgia's, you'd get great food and have a good time.

Besides serving good food at great prices, the bar side of the restaurant was a fun place to stop in or hang out. Many of the regulars had nicknames. There was "Gary the Carpenter," "Danny the Dancer," (he was a member of a German dance group) "Danny the Fence Wrecker," "Tom Thumb," and "Paul the Plumber." Paul tried to explain to Georgia that he was a steamfitter and not a plumber, but to no avail as the plumber tag stuck. Danny the Fence Wrecker earned his name because of an incident that happened one night when he left the restaurant. After getting into his vehicle, instead of putting it into reverse, he put it into drive, jumped the concrete stop and damaged a few slats in a stockade fence. No one saw him do it, but he felt so guilty he stayed away for about a month. When he finally came back, he confessed to Georgia what he had done and wanted to pay for it. The cost to repair it was less than five dollars, and Georgia refused to even tell him how much it would cost to pay for the damages. She respected his honesty and remorse, so instead she requested he sing his rendition of "Oh Danny Boy" as payment. I have his performance on tape and he should have been a professional—what a voice!

## THE PROPOSAL

Also around that time, I proposed marriage to Georgia in a knight's suit of shining armor on a white horse. Part of the procession would include a customer and friend, Kurt, who liked dressing up as Robin Hood, as he did on one occasion the previous year when we accompanied him to the Renaissance Fair in upstate New York. That occasion was not a happy experience for Georgia. She was not into "thee, thou, or fair maiden" Renaissance culture. It was a swelteringly hot day upstate with no breeze and that might have contributed to one of the very few times she did not enjoy herself, and I being a romantic, was taking a chance in choosing this method of a proposal.

So "Robin Hood," and four of his students dressed up as "merry men" to play heralding music as part of the procession. We assembled at Lucille's home, her friend and barmaid, who lived just around the corner from the restaurant. My excuse for not being around that day after school was that I had to attend a meeting. The white horse was supposed to be delivered there at 4:00 p.m., but didn't arrive until after 5:00 p.m. Needless to say, I was a little nervous, but the merry men practiced on their trumpets and trombones until the horse arrived, and we then proceeded down the block to her restaurant. Robin Hood led the group, followed by the merry men, and then me on the white horse. When she saw Kurt who was a social studies teacher,

*The Knight, the Merry Men, and Robin Hood*

dressed as Robin Hood, she thought he was enacting some skit with his students. But then she recognized me as I walked up to her after getting off the horse. I had a proposal speech written and rehearsed, but couldn't remember a single word so I just got down on one knee and asked if she would marry me. Everyone in the bar joined her outside on the steps, as well as other onlookers in the parking lot, to witness the event.

When she said yes, "Robin Hood" then surprised me as he read a proclamation that stated. "Let it be known throughout the realm of Lindenhurst, that on this day of June 1, 1989, the good knight Sir Joseph of McKasty has asked for the hand of Lady Georgette of Calogeras in marriage, and the fair maiden has joyously accepted. Let the entire realm rejoice at this celebration

*The procession to the restaurant*

of love." She often recounted in later years that when she said yes, she didn't say when, but it took only two years for us to wed.

*Above: The Knight, Georgia, and Robin Hood*

*Right: Georgia's acceptance*

I had told Ellie, her mother, about my intentions beforehand and my method of proposing. She asked what the ring looked like. Now, with all the plotting, planning, and preparation, I had never even thought about a ring. Ellie contacted my mother who provided me with a rhinestone one to give her. It passed the test for a while. Georgia thought it was the real thing, but about two weeks later she was informed about my failure to get a real diamond ring. That mistake was rectified within one month, with a beautiful twelve marquise diamond combination engagement and wedding ring. I was reminded several times in later years about that original rhinestone ring that I had gotten from my mother from a box of Cracker Jacks.

## JÄGER & MEISTER

I was lucky enough to be a teacher which allowed

**Proclamation**

Let it be known throughout the realm of Lindenhurst, that on this day of June 1st in the year of our Lord 1982, the good knight Sir Joseph of Mc Rasty has asked for the hand of Lady Georgette of Calogeras in marriage, and the faire maiden has joyously accepted.

Let the entire realm rejoice at this celebration of Love.

*The Proclamation*

me to have a lot of holidays and vacations to enjoy the fun lifetime ride with her. One of her distributors, Dieter, was the Dinkelacker Bier supplier. She hosted quite a few "Drink a Dink" parties. Dieter inherited Georgia's two goats, "Jäger" and "Meister," when the village wouldn't allow her to keep them on the restaurant property anymore. He owned a German restaurant and a farm upstate in Wyndam, New York. Because she had visitation rights, we visited the goats on occasion while staying at Dieter's, snowmobiling if it was in the winter, or just sightseeing in the summer time.

At Christmas, Dieter would turn his warehouse in Nassau County into a winter wonderland. He brought dozens of Christmas trees and erected them, undecorated throughout the warehouse, to make you feel as though you were in a forest in Germany. He had a stand set up to serve his Dinkelacker Bier and another to serve hot red wine. He had various other stands to serve you food as you strolled through the forest.

*Dieter with Jäger & Meister*

There was also German music, but the centerpiece was a nativity scene with live animals around the manger. I think there were lambs and ducks, and of course, Georgia's donated goats, Jäger and Meister.

On one of our trips to Germany, we visited Dieter's American restaurant called Zur Ranch Steakhouse. It was western themed, with a matching décor and served good old American steaks. Dieter was a person who also knew how to have a good time. He respected Georgia's entrepreneurship and we always enjoyed his company and his events. We were invited to ride on his float in New York

*Georgia on Dinkelacker float*

City's Steuben Day Parade. She wore her "dirndl" (a traditional German dress) and I wore my lederhosen as we drank his Dinkelacker Bier on a beautiful fall day riding on that float up Fifth Avenue.

## NEWFOUND BROTHER

During our courtship years, another one of our excursions was a cruise to Alaska in July. I told my biological father about our plans to go on this cruise a few months before the trip. He said he had someone up there he would like me to meet. He never got around to giving me contact information at that time, but a week before we left, he called me. He gave me the person's name and phone number and said, "by the way, he is your brother." At forty-seven years old, I found out that I have another brother! Well, I called Kevin, my newly-found brother, before we embarked, and arranged to meet him in Anchorage. I found another brother and Georgia made another friend. Kevin and his wife, Janice, made it down to our wedding a few years later.

That was another fun cruise when, at one stop, we took a helicopter ride to the top of a glacier and walked around on it. At first I was a little apprehensive after getting into the helicopter. Now, being an ex-paratrooper, I'm not afraid of flying in one, but being the heaviest of our group, I was designated to sit up front with the pilot as Georgia sat in the back with the other tourists. I was a little concerned because our pilot was this beautiful, young, blonde, female who didn't look old enough to be able to handle this chopper. Yes, I stereotyped her as a "dumb blonde," but she did an excellent job as we lifted off in formation with five other choppers, just like you see in the old MASH series on television. We flew at about one hundred feet or so above the glacier and got a bird's eye view of the crevices, rock, and dirt lines showing it to be a slow moving "river" of ice.

After a twenty-minute flight up the "ice river," one by one, each chopper lands in formation on a vast flat area about half-way up the glacier. All tourists disembark, the choppers leave, and we're free to roam about until they return an hour or so later with the next group. Even though we're on a glacier, it was almost tee-shirt weather, because this was July. One of the things that fascinated Georgia was the pockets of crystal clear water with a rock in each one. The sun heated the rocks which melted the water under them to form the pockets. Some were over three feet deep, with the rock appearing to be only inches below the surface. Also, up river there was a gushing waterfall caused by the spring/summer melt that disappeared under the

*On the glacier*

plateau area we were standing on.

Each day we did something different: one day we fished for salmon, on another we navigated whitewater rapids in a ten-person raft, and still on another day we paddled a twenty-plus-person canoe across a mountain lake to enjoy freshly smoked salmon in the crisp, clear air after reaching the other side. Now, smoked salmon tastes good at any time, but that day it tasted exceptionally great. When the cruise ended, we took an extended tour on a two day train ride through Denali State Park with an overnight stay in a lodge in the park. It was awesome. The train had glass-domed cars so you could really enjoy the beauty of Alaska. The views were breathtaking and majestic, from bear and American bald eagle sightings to Dall sheep and caribou. The train traveled through the heart of the park where there are no signs of civilization, no roads, no buildings, no telephone poles—just those tracks transporting us through this wonderland.

*White water rafting*

Georgia and I made a return trip to my newly-found brother Kevin and his wife, Janice's home in Wasilla, Alaska a few years later—a lot of fun again and lots of laughs. In our group this time was Georgia and I, my father, my brother Willie and his wife Kathy, my half-brother Peter, and his then-wife Diane. One day

*Canoeing across a mountain lake*

while up there we decided to do some salmon fishing. It's called combat fishing because scores and scores of fishermen are lined up on both sides of a stream or river, almost elbow to elbow, all fishing for salmon. You could see all the salmon swimming right on by, but they are not taking the bait because their only interest is in getting upstream to spawn. So someone came up with the idea to tell Diane that the best chance to catch any was to bait your hook with a marshmallow. So she put one on her hook, gave it a try and cast it into the river. All the other fishermen were wondering what the hell she was doing, as our group was laughing their butts off. None of our group caught any fish even with an airboat ride to another spot, but it was still fun, with seaplane rides and a day of halibut fishing.

What a day that was! We had to be dockside by 5:30 a.m. The fifty foot boat left the dock at 6:00 a.m. for a three hour ride to the fishing area. It reminded me of a Victory at Sea television episode—one of those WWII naval documentaries about navy missions showing ships going through very rough seas. Out of our party of ten, Georgia, Kevin, Janice, their daughter Leah, and I were the only ones who didn't throw up because of those seas. While brothers and sisters-in-law were heaving over the railing, the mates were amazed as Georgia was having a beer in the cabin. She even had to retrieve my father's false teeth from a "buddy" bucket he had used because of his sea sickness. She was a trooper! We reached our fishing spot around 9:00 a.m. in three hundred eighty-five feet of water just before the tidal change. The mates would bait the hook, put on a four pound sinker, cast the line, make sure it bottomed out, and then hand us the rod. Within minutes we had a fish on the hook and reeled in over four hundred feet of line with a good-sized Halibut. It was quite a workout, as the mates likened it to hauling up a piece of plywood staying level to the ocean bottom. After we reeled it to the top, the mates would haul it aboard, blackjack it, re-bait our hook, cast, grab bottom, and hand us the rod again. Within minutes, we had another hit and it was reeling time again. When we started fishing at 9:00 a.m., the lines were drifting to the right at almost a forty-five degree angle. In less than one hour, the lines were straight down, and shortly after that they were drifting at a forty-five degree angle to the left. That's how fast and strong the tidal change was.

After we caught our limit of twenty fish (two per person), the captain weighed anchor and took us to a sheltered cove to try for some big ones since we could have gotten six more because they also allow two for each crew member. The cove had calm waters, and was bordered by steep, lush, green mountains with patches of snow here and there, and some grazing Dall sheep. The scenery made you feel like you were part of a painting. The air was clean, clear, and crisp and helped everyone recover from their Victory at Sea ordeal while the four brothers with their wives did some bonding. It was Georgia's idea to do this trip, taking Kevin up on his offer to come up and visit anytime.

## ELLIE'S BACKYARD

Some nights during those courting years, before we left the restaurant to head home, we would stop in for a quick visit to see her mother, Ellie, who lived in the house right behind the restaurant. Ellie had a dog named Pookie that Georgia acquired from a former employee. With her busy schedule and lifestyle, Georgia thought it would be better for the dog and good for Ellie if Ellie took care of him. Georgia wanted to show me a trick where Pookie would jump up onto her lap when she called "upsie." But when she said it that night, Pookie ran over and jumped up onto my lap. Many times after school, and before I would catch up with her at the restaurant, I would visit Ellie and take the dog for a walk. I guess he got more used to me than Georgia, causing him to jump into my lap rather than

*Ellie & Pookie*

hers that particular time. I was lucky, both her mother and her dog liked me.

We had quite a few parties in Ellie's backyard, including several pig roasts. At one of those roasts, I had to build a four by five by four foot high barbeque. It was an enclosure made up of metal fence stakes and turkey wire wrapped in tin foil with a cover to contain the heat. The spit was a one and three-eighths inch wooden closet pole with a car steering wheel attached being supported by four by four inch posts. Because it took so long to roast a ninety pound pig, we had to start the night before. We arranged a schedule of two-hour shifts with volunteers of regular customers from the

*Pete & Gigi tending the pig*

restaurant. Whoever had the early morning shift didn't do their job of making sure to rotate the steering wheel a quarter turn every fifteen minutes. The closet pole we used as a skewer burned and broke into two pieces resulting in the pig falling into the fire. After salvaging and cleaning it, I had to reassemble the two separate pieces of pig onto what was left of the longer part of the skewer. But to do so, the top half of the pig was facing up while the bottom end was facing down. It was the only way to fit it onto the shortened skewer and fit it in between the relocated posts. Well, even though it fell into the charcoal fire, had to be cleaned, and looked like a freak of nature, everyone said it did taste good. On future pig roasts, we determined it would be wiser to have two-person teams on each shift so no one would fall asleep at the wheel. We also had a log splitting contest at that BBQ and Georgia's friend and bartender, Dale, did a good job of besting a lot of the men.

Georgia enjoyed having a party once in a while in Ellie's backyard as it got her mother involved in some of her fun activities, like the cucumber-in-a-bottle contest. The only rule was that it had to be grown in any size alcoholic container that wasn't cut or altered for it to

*Above: Gigi & Barbara judging an entry extracted from a beer can*

*Right: Cucumber-in-a-bottle entries*

grow in. There were prizes for various categories such as the largest or the weirdest. Pete and Gigi grew one in a beer can. We had to cut the can open with a pair of snips and it won a prize for being the weirdest. "Gary the Carpenter" won first place out of almost two dozen entries because his was in a liquor bottle. My stepfather, Mike, also won a prize for having grown one that was larger than Gary's, but he had grown it in a plastic five gallon water jug.

## GERMANY AGAIN

On our second trip to Germany in '92, Georgia arranged for a bus to bring the twenty of us to the airport. Again, good times and good memories as we toured Germany in five rented Mercedes cars. We tied white handkerchiefs to our antennas so the lead car could see if the convoy was still together. We stayed in Onkel's hometown for two or three days and saw the lamppost his tongue got stuck on one winter during his childhood. We visited the house where he grew up and the present owners invited us in for a tour. A lot of fond memories for Onkel, thanks to Georgia.

One member of our group, Mike, who owned a few sports bar restaurants on Long Island, drove on his own one night, to an American Military Base about fifty kilometers away to pick up his son who was stationed there. He got lost on his way back to our hotel, so he found a cab, showed the driver a matchbook from the hotel, and asked the driver how much it would cost to go back to that hotel. He then hired him to lead the way back, and Mike followed in his car. Those were the days before GPS. Mike also distinguished himself by getting ejected from a local casino for improper behavior, but

*Joe, Georgia, Carol, and Chet*

redeemed himself after his wife, Peggy, hit it big on a machine in another nearby casino.

We traveled through a good portion of Germany and briefly rode into Austria. We climbed the steps to the tower of the Cathedral in Koln, we sailed on the Rhine and on the lake at Tegernsee, we drank beer at the Hofbrau House in München, and we took a tour of Beck's Brewery. That Beck's tour started at around 9:00 a.m., and we figured we would get a sampling of beer at the end of it. Instead, as soon as all twenty of us entered the building, a bartender was pouring glasses of beer, letting the head settle in each glass as he then poured another one without spilling a single drop. As the beer in each glass settled, he again poured into each one, sometime three or four times, until the head rose above the rim about a half inch with a little dimple right in the middle where the last drop went in. We were escorted to a table set with a breakfast spread of cold cuts, cheese, bread and rolls, and of course, all those perfectly poured beers, drinking as much as we wanted. After breakfast, which lasted about an hour, we then toured the immaculate premises of the brewery at a leisurely pace because we'd already had our sampling. Thank you Georgia! It was through her connection with her beer distributor that we were able to do this tour.

*Onkel, Carol, and Georgia*

# CHAPTER

## II

# The Wedding

After a whirlwind courtship of five years, we finally got married on the Fourth of July, 1991. She claimed to have picked that date so that I wouldn't forget our anniversary. We held the affair at her restaurant with the Mayor of Lindenhurst performing the ceremony. Her mother, Ellie, died just six weeks prior to the wedding, but she decided to proceed with it anyway, knowing that Ellie would have wanted that. Naturally, it was quite an affair. We had a huge forty by sixty foot tent erected in the rear parking lot to accommodate all the guests. I believe there were over two hundred. Smaller ones were set up for the DJ and the German band, the food, and the bar. Originally,

*The white carriage*

Georgia was going to oversee the cooking and serving, but catering business relatives on her father's side from New Jersey volunteered to take over those duties. My mother hired a horse-drawn white carriage to deliver Georgia and Lucille, her maid of honor, with her dog riding shotgun, from the village docks to the wedding site. Sonny, my best friend and best man at my first wedding, was again my best man for this wedding.

Naturally, the wedding was a fantastic event. Purple was her favorite color and there were hundreds of purple and white balloons all over the place. I wore my white tuxedo with a purple cummerbund and bow tie, and the wedding cake also was white and purple. After she arrived in the carriage, her Uncle Bud and Onkel Herman escorted her down the aisle to the ceremony site where they gave her away. With all the planning for this event, we never practiced the ceremony part, but we muddled our way through it. After we exchanged our vows, another party immediately began with her relatives from Florida, my new-found brother Kevin from Alaska, his wife Janice, all the aunts, uncles, and cousins from both sides along with friends and co-workers as all enjoyed dancing to current popular and

*Her sign on the wedding day*

German songs including the "Chicken Dance." Our friends, Helmut and Regina even flew in from Germany for the occasion.

Georgia also hired a belly dancer for the occasion and that was a big hit. It takes a special person to do that, for what bride would want to hire a belly dancer to perform, which would take some of the attention away from the bride on her big day. Again on tape, it shows quite a few of the men dancing with the belly dancer, with a friend of mine even trying to take some of the dollars from her rather than trying to stuff money into her outfit. It was a beautiful affair on a

*The Beautiful Bride*

beautiful day; and she truly was a beautiful bride.

Her dress was made by Connie, who came from Germany and was a friend of Onkel and therefore a friend of Georgia's. Connie owned a bridal shop and did a fantastic job on her gown, but wouldn't accept any money for it—truly a good friend. But a year later, Georgia was able to reciprocate for that favor. Connie put her two sons through college—Gunther becoming an oral surgeon and Robert becoming a stock trader. But she always felt ashamed about her lack of a high school diploma. I volunteered to tutor her and had to encourage her not to give up when she encountered the math and algebra segment. She persevered and after a lot of studying, took the two-day tests. She anxiously awaited the results and was reluctant to open the envelope when it finally arrived, thinking that she was not going to pass. She passed everything and was awarded her GED diploma! She was a happy and proud woman. So, to celebrate the occasion, Georgia

*Above: Connie's graduation*

*Right: Gunther and Robert*

hosted a graduation party for her at the restaurant with her husband, two sons, and a bunch of her friends equally proud of her. Thank you, Georgia; it was one of the proudest and happiest days of Connie's life.

## OUR DREAM HOUSE

Around this time we also bought our dream house down in the Florida Keys. We had frequently vacationed in Key West, Key Largo, or at Franky and Kiki's house on Little Torch Key. They were friends of Georgia and were indirectly related to Onkel Herman through marriage. We would hook up with my son, Joseph, who lived down there working as a carpenter and fisherman. He would take us fishing and then cook us an excellent dinner from our catch and the stone crab claws from his traps. Stone crab claws taste better than lobster. And the best thing about taking them is, after you remove them from the trap, measure to make sure they're of legal size, and break off their claw, you throw them back into the sea and they will grow another claw! Talk about recycling!

We told Joseph that if he ever came across a good deal on a house, he should let us know. The year after our wedding, he informed us that the contractor he was working for wanted to move back up north to, I think Michigan, and the house he was working on was for sale. It was partially built, with the exterior concrete walls constructed to halfway up the window cut-outs on the second floor, which only had a subfloor. It was a two bedroom, two bathroom home on a canal in Big Pine Key on a cul-de-sac. We liked the site; the price was right, so we bought it and hired my son to finish the construction. He did a beautiful job, but we made a mistake of telling him we were not in a rush to have it completed.

Because Joseph took so long to work on the house, and I think because Georgia thought he was going to move in, she wanted to fire him. He did sheetrock part of the garage for his cot and his workbench (which was red tagged as a violation by the building department) and he did store a lot of his belongings in another part of the downstairs storage area. But I told her that he was not going to be moving in, and it would be difficult to get another contractor to finish the job at a reasonable price or to complete the work any quicker. This was one of the few times I disagreed with her and I did not want to fire him at this stage of the construction. It's a difficult task to get construction workers to work down in the Keys. They'd rather go fishing than work, and quite often do, resulting in construction delays.

In 1994, one week after school was finished, we

headed down to the Keys in our motor home. Since it was about 95% completed, I decided to stay the whole summer to work on the house and Georgia flew back to New York to take care of the restaurant.

## TROUBLE IN PARADISE

Joseph showed up about one week after I started working on the house. I thought he was finally coming to work on it, but he was only there to pick up his stuff that had accumulated in the storage area. I asked him when he was going to continue working on the house. He replied that he was not. I asked why and he said, "I can't work on a job where my work is not appreciated." He finished loading his stuff and left. I was stunned. I had no idea why he felt that way. That's the last time we spoke to each other, although I have tried to reconcile with him a few times since, but to no avail. One time was when I asked his girlfriend, Nadine, what I could do to reconcile and she said, "He does like to have a beer." I went right down from her beauty shop to the Square Grouper to get two beers and went to his shop which was right behind it. I asked him if it was time to talk and he said no. I turned around, walked out, and dumped both bottles just outside his overhead door. I guess he is more stubborn than I am. Up until last year, it had been twenty years since he had last spoken to me.

Permits and inspections are required for many phases during the construction process before you can get a Certificate of Occupancy; probably more so down here in the Keys. I successfully got all of them, except for one, when I finished working on the house that summer. I left to go back north the week before school began. I settled in and started school. At the end of the second week of school, I came home and found that Georgia had moved out. When she finally contacted me a day later, she informed me that she wanted a divorce. WHAM! It felt like I was hit across the chest with a two by four. It hurt! And she never said why. I guess it was because she thought I was sticking up for Joseph too much. I guess Joseph thought I was sticking up for Georgia and now neither one wants me—not as a husband, nor as a father. I moved out of Georgia's house the next day, getting a hotel room for two weeks until I rented an apartment, and then bought a condo forty miles away. Thus began our seven year "intermission."

During our intermission, I traded my Harley

Davidson Sportster for a green and black 1997 Ultra Classic Touring Bike, joined the Harley Owners Group (HOG) and did a lot of riding. It helped heal the wounds of the divorce. I turned over my half of the house in Florida, the boat, and the RV to her. I didn't care about keeping any of them. We had a prenuptial agreement regarding the restaurant because that was her baby. I left the marriage with less than I came into it with, as she gained those assets. I told her lawyer that she could have everything that was in joint ownership and I didn't even hire my own attorney. The uncontested divorce was granted very quickly.

I hooked up with a girl named Janet, who was a school bus driver which allowed us to spend a lot of vacation time together. She was a good lady, but I did miss Georgia. John, a friend of Georgia's and mine, attempted on several occasions to get us back together again. One time he invited Janet and me to a gala Fourth of July party at his house. He lived in a mansion on a canal and had Georgia cater the event. Another time he invited me to meet him for some cocktails after school at Tellers restaurant, a fancy upscale place in Islip, Long Island. But Georgia was the only one there instead because he had invited only her to meet him there. We talked for a little while at each of those occasions, but nothing came of it. She was seeing a guy named Lenny, and I guess she was happy with that situation.

In 1999, John called and offered to pay for my airfare to Key West for a one week stay with him, his wife, Chris, Georgia, and her friend, Dale. I really liked my job at BOCES, being a special education vocational teacher, and having over two hundred sick days accumulated, I still wouldn't take a week off. I did tell him, though, that I would come down for the weekend leaving right after school on Friday, and leave there Sunday afternoon to go back home. He said he would reserve a room for me at the Galleon where they were all staying. Their two bedroom suite was an exchange week from a timeshare that Georgia and I had bought during our early courtship years.

I arrived in Key West after midnight, having left Long Island so late in the day and having had to drive from Miami to Key West. I tried to check into my room but the desk was closed. I wandered around and looked in some of the local bars and restaurants to try to find my friends, but had no luck. Finally I went back to the resort and sat on a bench thinking I might be sleeping there. About fifteen minutes later, Georgia and Dale came strolling by—Dale a little tipsy. After telling them about not being able to get into my room, they invited me up to their room. We put Dale to bed, and Georgia and I went out for a few cocktails, returning an hour or so later. I ended up having to sleep in the same bed with both of them. Georgia and I did some communicating with nothing being resolved, though she seduced me as I slept on the pull out couch in the living room late Saturday night. The following week I had a discussion with Janet expressing my desire to break off our relationship. I could understand her pain and sorrow and wound up staying with her because I knew how it felt. We lasted another two years, but we finally did separate. I moved out of my condo in the summer of 2001, giving Jan time to relocate while I stayed at my son Michael's house in Lindenhurst for a few months.

## THE RECONCILIATION

During that time I reconnected with Georgia and we reconciled. She had sold her house in Amityville and was living in the apartment over the restaurant. I was in the process of retiring by working thirty school days and then getting terminal leave pay by using one hundred fifty of my two hundred plus unused sick days. Georgia was in the process of selling her restaurant building. The restaurant business itself was not for sale. I don't think she could bear the thought of someone else running her "baby." Little by little, during our intermission, she sold off parts of her properties around the restaurant—first the two houses behind it, then the house alongside it, and now the last piece, the building itself—all to the boatyard down the street. They have since leased it out five times as a bar and restaurant, and no one has yet been as successful as she was.

During the last thirty days or so before the closing, it was party time every day and night. Georgia had a CD that I believe a Spaten Bier Distributor had given to her with a song entitled "Hey Baby." It's a redo of a Bruce Channel original hit song from 1961, done by a German band. When played, it puts everyone in a party mood. Georgia got everyone to change words so they were singing it to her to be their friend, instead of their "girl." I still kept it personal asking if she'd be my girl. It seemed like she must have played that song twenty to thirty times a day, every day, during that last month. I got so tired of hearing it, I thought about having someone put it in a skeet shooting machine as I yelled "pull" so I could shoot the disc. It was a happy time and it was a sad time, but it was the best way she could say goodbye to her baby, Georgia's German Restaurant.

Georgia was now living with me in Manorville and one week after the closing, we went on a vacation to Cozumel. It was at a time-share unit that we had bought the first time we were married. We spent five days in Cozumel and five days in Cancun. On the very first day in Cozumel we went to Señor Frog's, which was always a happy and festive place. Within the first ten minutes, we heard the Spaten Bier version of "Hey Baby." Oh, no! I thought I had escaped having to listen to it at home, and would have sworn she was responsible for having it played. Who would have thought that an oldie American song sung by a German band would be so popular in Mexico. But because it's such a happy tune, it's still played often even today, to put people in a happy mood and to get them up and dancing. This was another video moment, and I gave my camera to someone on the dance floor to tape Georgia and I having fun again.

This time in Cozumel was special because this was where we had started our time-share experience. During the first chapter of our courtship we had come here for a few hours while on a cruise around the Western Caribbean. The hotel allowed cruise ship passengers to swim at the lagoon in front of their place. There were three pools and two bars located on a beautiful calm sandy beach lagoon setting with sloping paths leading to rocky outcrops, and a fantastic view of crystal clear blue and turquoise waters. One could actually see the small single engine plane that was used in a James Bond movie anchored to the bay bottom in about thirty feet of water just outside the lagoon. We fell for the sales pitch by a lovely little señorita named Margarita and bought a time-share because we really loved it there. Georgia and Margarita hit it off very well—so much so that we were invited to Margarita's baby's christening a year or two later when we happened to be there at that time.

During our intermission, they transferred the time-share to Cancun and Georgia didn't like it as much. Cozumel was more laid back and not as hectic with night life as Cancun. Georgia said she had even tried to give the time-share away during our intermission.

I'm glad she was unsuccessful because we have used it many times since then—mostly in Cancun. The Park Royal in Cancun is an all-inclusive destination with free food and drinks. We spent a good deal of our time at the hotel just vegging out. Once in a while we would go to Carlos & Charlie's or to Señor Frog's or just take the bus to town. On many of our trips we also invited family and/or friends to share the fun with us as we reserved the Presidential Suite to accommodate them—again, fun and relaxation were the main objectives. The year 2001 was the beginning of the Joey III era; Georgia's first husband was Joe I, and I was Joe II during our first marriage.

Damn it! Why did she have to be right? Thinking back, another sign of her illness was that she was frequently out of breath. In addition to difficulties resulting from attempted "long walks," Georgia would sometimes have problems breathing just sitting in her chair or even in bed at night. She would always need to have the fan on at night, to make it easier for her to breathe. I kept "suggesting" that she go see a doctor. Since no one could tell her what to do, she refused to go.

Besides shortness of breath, some other medical

issues included: no energy, constipation, no appetite, a skin rash, and who knows what else. Her actions and words indicated a slowdown of the body and an awareness of her leaving us. Occasionally in the last year or two, she would say that she was going to die before me. I didn't want to hear that. When her cousins, Maryann and her daughters Jamie and Marissa visited us at Christmas those last two years, Georgia gave them some jewelry to be sure they received what she wanted them to have. We also retrieved other jewelry from our safe deposit box so she could designate who should get those pieces as well. I didn't even know at the time that she had, in one of those Crown Royal velvet-like bags, fifty one hundred dollar bills in six separate sealed envelopes, each designated for six specific children of some of her close friends. During our intermission she even took out a million dollar irrevocable life insurance policy, with an annual premium of over ten thousand dollars listing her nephew Peter as the beneficiary. When we discussed this after our reconciliation, Georgia said at that time she felt as though she wasn't going to be around in the near future—again, something I dismissed because I didn't want to hear it. She even designated who should get certain monkeys from her vast collection, saying if something should happen to her, this or that monkey goes to so and so.

# Maimou and Her Monkeys

**A**h—Her monkeys!! When she was a child, her father would call her Maimou, which is Greek for monkey. She enjoyed the name until she saw one at the Bronx Zoo. Her mother took her there one day and pointed out a monkey stating, "Look, there's a maimou." It was an orangutan and Georgia didn't like the looks of it. She declared that she was not a maimou, but the name stuck anyway.

During our courtship years, I had an older forty-eight foot Chris-Craft boat that we traded in for a new thirty-two foot Sea Ray. Naturally, we named it "Maimou." We bought it in Port Jefferson on the North Shore of Long Island, and our maiden voyage was to bring it to her home in Amityville on the South Shore. It was another fun and exciting day as we cruised along Long Island Sound, down the East River, and to the Statue of Liberty. Awesome! It was breathtaking as we first saw the statue after passing under

Maimou (the boat)

the Brooklyn Bridge while checking out the projects (housing units) where Georgia had grown up in lower Manhattan. After seeing the statue from a distance, it slowly grew larger as we approached it until we were so close that it towered over us. What a magnificent view from the water and being so close was awesome. Georgia's customer and friend, Lou, who was a bay constable, helped us navigate the waters on that trip. We had that boat for many years and made trips to Atlantic City, Block Island, Fire Island, and also had numerous fishing outings on it.

Prior to our courtship, I had this monkey puppet. I could put my arm up through his back with my hand operating his head and my fingers working his mouth. His arms would wrap around my neck and his legs would wrap around my waist attaching with Velcro as he "sat" on my other hand and appeared to be hanging onto me. His name was Mickey and he usually only came out twice a year—St. Patrick's Day and again on New Year's Eve—and only after I had had a few drinks. His drink of choice back then was Lambrusco, a sweet red wine, but he also drank anything else with a straw in it. He was a big hit with the ladies and naturally, Georgia loved him too.

It wasn't until after our reconciliation that she got into collecting hundreds of monkeys and monkey-related items. Our neighbors, Jim and Beata across the canal have a daughter, Lexie, whose job was to take a monkey inventory during our Christmas party each year. Georgia saved each of those inventory records and had planned to give them back to Lexie as part of her wedding gift when she married. At last count, there were over three hundred monkeys, or monkey-related items in Georgia's collection.

## THE PARTYING MONKEYS

She has one monkey that plays cymbals, two that jump rope, and many others that sing or dance. Occasionally, we would go to Key West and she would bring some of the monkey troops with her to entertain Beverly, Julia, and Bonnie—bartenders at Sloppy Joe's—and their customers. Beverly made sure that Georgia's favorite monkey, Maimou, got a drink served in a shot glass with a straw so that he could have fun too. There was usually a one-man band for entertainment during the

*Some of the monkey crew*

day and she would put the cymbal-playing monkey and the rope-jumping monkeys on the stage while the entertainer was playing. One time at Hog's Breath Saloon, she put the cymbal-playing monkey on Barry Cuda's piano and the two rope-jumping ones on the stage. Barry, who plays honky tonk piano is a one-man entertainment show. He went along with it and played his music in time with the monkeys, even pausing when one of the rope-jumping ones fell over and took a while to recover, resuming play when the monkey got back up. Again, this was another video moment captured.

Linda, one of her Florida Keys yard "sale-ing" buddies is a real estate agent. On one of Linda's walk-through visits prior to a closing, she was checking out all the rooms and closets, and came across a twenty-six inch tall, dark, bronze monkey lamp sitting on a floor in a closet. Its lampshade tail was over half that height sticking straight up without a shade. She inquired if she could have it and was told she could. She knew immediately that she was going to give it to Georgia. She couldn't wait until she could and naturally, Georgia was elated to adopt another "homeless" monkey. Linda apologized for not having a shade for the lamp. It turned

out that two weeks earlier, while
"sale-ing" with another friend Trish,
Georgia bought a small Tiffany-style
lampshade that was a perfect match
for it. At that time it had no intended
use, and she didn't know why she
bought it. But now, that lamp and
shade have been united, and it is
perched on a pedestal at the top of
our stairway landing.

*Linda's monkey lamp*

She met another monkey lover
while out garage "sale-ing" and
Georgia formed another strong friendship. She had a
bolt of monkey fabric in her car that she had purchased
at a previous yard sale. While at this particular sale,
she asked if they had any monkeys. Richard, who was
running the sale, replied that if he did have any monkeys,
he wouldn't sell any of them because he loved them, too.
Georgia then showed him that bolt of monkey fabric
she had just bought two weeks ago at a yard sale and
was looking to cover a few ottomans her father bought
many years ago. Richard told her he was an upholsterer
and could do that for her. She gave the job to him and

added another friend to her long expanding list. In the following years, Richard attended many functions at our house as well as inviting us to many at his home. Many years later, Richard and his significant other, Walter, gave her a monkey chandelier when they had to move into smaller quarters. It wouldn't fit into their new surroundings. They also gave her a Victorian style chair—naturally upholstered with monkey fabric.

## THE CHANDELIER

We didn't know it then, but later saw that same chandelier at Fast Buck Freddy's in Key West selling for $1200. The one they had given her had one of three monkeys, which resembled the flying monkeys in the Wizard of Oz, completely broken off. We took it up north with us and after settling in; I started repairing it one morning at around 9:00 a.m. as it first had to be rewired. Each upright extended arm held a candle-like light with a small shade. A wire ran down through each arm into the body, through the leg, and into the base. Gratefully, only one wire had to be replaced, and it took me only half an hour to do it the first time. But upon testing it before I reattached it to the base, I found no current

*The chandelier*

going through it. I pulled the wire back out thinking I might have chafed the insulation off the wire as I snaked it through. I didn't. My second attempt to snake another wire through took until 10:00 p.m. because of the almost ninety degree angle of the arm to the body. I guess I was lucky the first time. It wasn't until after I went to a local bait shop and bought some one hundred pound test fishing line, that I was finally able to snake the wire through. Georgia kept telling me to give it up, but I was determined to get it ready for a professional licensed electrician to install it over the midway landing of our condo stairway. She took pictures and sent them to Richard and Walter who were now living in Fort Wayne, Indiana. Again, this was another happy day for Georgia after seeing it finally installed.

There has been only one occasion where a monkey was ejected from an establishment. Georgia was carrying her forty-two inch Curious George through the crowded bar area into the dining room where he accidently hit and knocked over one of those high back bar chairs next to a high table. The owner of the restaurant, which was then called "Parrotdise," came over to our table and told Georgia the monkey had to go. It was the first meeting of some organization at this place, and the owner wanted to make a good impression on them. I guess he showed them he wouldn't tolerate any monkey business. Georgia felt insulted and embarrassed as I had to put the monkey back into our vehicle, and we rarely went back to that restaurant.

## EX-WIVES AND COOKIES

Another example of how Georgia got along with other people is when my first ex-wife, Nancy, came down to

Florida. She picked up two of our grandkids, Coralynn and Quinn, and took them to Disney World for a week. Then Nancy came down to the Keys to stay with my son, Joseph and his girlfriend, Nadine. After a few days there, she asked if she and the kids could stay here at our house because it was a little crowded over at my son's. Georgia had no problem with that and all three stayed here with us. We took them out fishing and boating. I again had another video moment when I recorded Quinn showing us with his arms and hands how he had learned to tie his shoelaces. On another trip from Long Island down to the Keys, Nancy picked up our grandson, Kyle, in Orlando, and we all went to Sloppy Joe's. It has to be one of the busiest bars anywhere and when we sat down at the bar I told Beverly, the barmaid, to give my two ex-wives a drink on me. She looked at me like I was crazy. We had to explain that, as Georgia and I had not yet remarried, they were in fact both my ex-wives. Georgia took it very well and laughed as we proceeded to have that drink.

Another episode involving a Key West outing occurred a little while after Georgia had made some big chocolate chip cookies. Georgia was an excellent cook and she gave me one to taste after they cooled off. That cookie was not so good. I was reluctant to tell her, but finally did let her know, whereupon she agreed and tried to figure out what went wrong in the process of making them. It was the only time I can recall, that something she cooked or baked, did not turn out good. She never did figure out what went wrong. One afternoon, about three weeks later, we were in Key West and stopped at Alonzo's Oyster Bar, where we enjoyed a few half-price cocktails and appetizers during their happy hour. After leaving there, we walked on Duval Street and passed a little coffee shop where some large chocolate chip cookies were displayed in their window. Georgia exclaimed, "There are the cookies I tried to make you!" We decided to go in and give one a taste test.

It was the first time in all the years we had gone down to Key West that we went into a coffee shop. I ordered one cookie and a small coffee and Georgia ordered a double espresso. It took a while for me to work on that cookie, which was good, so Georgia ordered another double espresso. The girl behind the counter asked her if she was trying to get high, to which Georgia replied, "No, I just like espresso." When we finished and got our check for those three coffees and one cookie, it was more than what we paid for cocktails and appetizers at Alonzo's. But, it gave us something to laugh about as we headed back up to Big Pine. We watched a little TV and went to bed around 10:00 p.m. At 12:30 p.m., she was still talking and I finally had to say, "Georgia, shut up." She then realized that having had two double espressos in the evening was not a good move. If she did order a double one after that, it was only one, and early in the day.

## "SALE-ING"

She enjoyed garage and/or yard "sale-ing." Being directionally challenged, (easily getting lost) she seldom drove and usually went with friends who chauffeured her around, both on Long Island and in the Keys, and also got them hooked on "sale-ing." Up north, she had Sue and Jenna as yard sale buddies and down in the Keys she had Linda, Trish or Betty. She usually wore her "Georgia's German Restaurant" shirt or jacket and enjoyed meeting people who had eaten there. There were even some restaurant patrons down here in the Keys, and they all commented on how good the food at

"Georgia's" was. It really impressed the new friends who were chauffeuring her around and had never been to her restaurant. Once in a while, I would get a phone call to meet the yard sale team with my truck to bring back another good find that was too big for them to fit into their car.

*The Knight's Suit*

One of Georgia's good finds was a full size knight's suit of shining armor. Originally it was used as an attention getter to lure customers into a novelty shop in Key West. It was mounted on a dolly and rolled in and out of the shop daily. The store closed and the owner held a yard sale for all the items from the store. Georgia called me as soon as she saw it and asked if I'd be interested in coming to take a look. I drove there and looked it over. They had an original price of $400 on it. It was a little beat up with some dings and rusted rivets, so I offered them $50 for it. They refused my offer saying they would only accept $100. I declined and left. Later that day I told her I should have accepted their offer and should have paid the $100. Since it was too late to go back that day, she said we could go back during the week and tell them that we'll pay their price for it. We went back twice during the week, but nobody was ever home. I figured we had missed out on that one. But Georgia contacted them later and bought it without my knowledge. Around this same time she was having some periodontal work done and had a lot of stitches in her mouth. Some of the stitches were loosening and she asked me to pull them out. I told her I couldn't do it because I was afraid of hurting her. She said that she would call the dentist and have him do it. I thought she left to have that done. About one hour after she left there was a knock on the door. I went downstairs and opened the door to see her, the knight, and a friend, Rowboat Bob, standing there. Here I had thought we'd missed out on getting that knight, but Georgia found a way to get it. That friend, Rowboat Bob, is another story.

## ROWBOAT BOB

Georgia tagged Bob and his wife Chris as Rowboat Bob and Chris. We met them upon returning from a fishing trip on our pontoon boat. We took some friends, Franky and Kiki, to the Gulf—about seven miles out through a lot of shallow water areas. Franky knew which way to go most of the time. After we caught enough fish, we headed back in. About halfway back, I saw this rowboat off to our right heading toward us as fast as it could be rowed, and it was on a collision course with us. Bob was doing the rowing and Chris in a yellow rain coat was bailing out the boat. I slowed our boat down as I neared them, and stopped when we were alongside, asking if there was a problem. Bob explained that the engine had malfunctioned and only worked in reverse. They also had been out in the Gulf and had been trying for hours to get back in. But getting back that day meant going against the southerly winds and going in reverse meant waves breaking over the transom allowing water into the boat. Chris looked a little worn out from all the bailing out she had been doing. We threw them a line and towed them back in, dropping off Franky and Kiki on the way in.

Bob and Chris were renting a place for a three month stay here in the Keys. When we got them to their place, Bob tried to give me some cash, and I told him, "No way." Georgia and Chris struck up a quick friendship and we were having some event at our house the following week so we invited them. I don't remember if it was Georgia's birthday (which she declared a national holiday), a sauerkraut-making event, or a Polish party. But Bob and Chris have come to most of our parties since then, and we have gone to many of theirs. They also got their chance to repay us for the tow by giving us a $100 gift certificate at a local restaurant. And whenever they attended events at our house, Georgia would always introduce them as Rowboat Bob and Chris.

## HABANEROS

Some of those events included sauerkraut making and sauerkraut unveiling parties. Georgia also enjoyed canning. She canned habanero jellies, green jalapeño mixed with red peppers and garlic for a colorful presentation, and most importantly, sauerkraut. She did it all to give away as presents to those friends who really enjoyed them. It takes a special person to enjoy that jalapeño jelly and a fanatical hot pepper lover to be able to enjoy her habanero jelly. The heat produced by hot peppers is measured in Scoville units. Jalapeño peppers are rated between 2500 and 5000 Scoville units while the habanero pepper is rated between 100,000 and 300,000 Scoville units. She grew her own peppers, at one time growing over two hundred thirty-two pepper plants in a sixty by seventy foot garden behind the restaurant. One hundred of them were habanero pepper plants.

*Right: Georgia wearing peppers*

*Below: Sitting in a "hot" car*

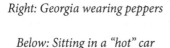

When the peppers ripened on those habanero plants, she envisioned starting up an enterprise producing "Georgia's Habanero Hot Sauce."

At first she started working on the crop of freshly picked habaneros in the basement of the restaurant. But as she was in the process of juicing them, the fumes permeated the whole place so much that she had to set up a table outside in the parking lot instead. It was right by a telephone pole with an electrical panel box that supplied power for her Oktoberfest events outside. After a few hours of using a juicer and blender (neither of which could be used for anything other than hot peppers after that), she wound up with containers of mulched seed and skin, and a two-gallon jar of lethal habanero liquid. She capped them and put them on top of a freezer chest down in the basement with the intention of placing them in the walk-in refrigerator. She went upstairs to get the key for the walk-in, got sidetracked, and never got to refrigerate them.

At 9:00 a.m. the next day, her chef called the house and told her something was wrong in the basement. We immediately went to the restaurant and saw the big bottle of juice was still on the chest freezer and it looked like it was bubbling and foaming. Georgia told him to bring it outside and set it on the blacktop. As he did, the lid popped off and sprayed juice mostly onto Georgia. She was hurting for a while from those habanero juice burns and that ended her hopes for that enterprise.

Another time, she held a contest to see who could grow the most habaneros on just one plant. Each contestant had to bring the whole plant in to show that they indeed were all on the same plant. There were only about six contestants (not too many people wanted to mess with or even touch habaneros), and Charlie (Zipper) won that contest with way over one hundred on his plant.

## SAUERKRAUT AND SODA BREAD

The sauerkraut-making parties started in the early years at the restaurant. Again, any reason was good reason to have a party. Franky, a brother to a son-in-law of Onkel Herman, supplied her with authentic German crocks of various sizes from one to thirty gallons, (big enough for a small child to take a bath in, but never did). It took two of us to lift the big one up even while it was empty. In all, she had about ten crocks. We would

*Kraut in crocks*

*Paul the Plumber tasting the kraut*

*Pookie checking out kraut—stomper in crock*

*Dale and her son Billy check the kraut*

get cases of cabbage (this past year we got three cases at a total weight of one hundred eighty pounds) and assign duties to each worker. Duties included: peel outer leaves, quarter each head, remove the cores, slice the quartered heads, weigh out five pound batches into trays, mix those batches with three tablespoons of pickling salt, then place and stomp them into the crocks. Those who didn't have an assignment, observed the others to make sure all of them were doing it right. As one pressed the cabbage down into the crock with a stomper, (or just one's fist), the juice would rise above the cabbage. We used a method where the cabbage didn't have to be skimmed every day. When the crock was filled to within a few inches from the top, we would weight it down with a tightly tied plastic bag, filled with brine in case of leakage. Then we sealed the crock with plastic wrap and taped it to make it airtight. Now it was time to party because the crocks were stored until it was time to unveil them and that provided the reason for another party in a few weeks. The temperature at which the crocks were stored determined when that party could take place. For example; if the temperature was seventy-five degrees, the sauerkraut would be ready in three weeks, at seventy degrees, it would take four weeks.

At the unveiling party, Georgia had a lot of work to do as the canning process began. She amassed quite a collection of mason jars from her yard "sale-ing" and used quite a few of them. After leaving the crocks, the sauerkraut now had to be boiled in batches for twenty minutes, packed into the jars, and then submerged in water in canning jars for another twenty minutes, making sure the jars and lids have also been sanitized in boiling water. The jars are then removed with special tongs and placed on the kitchen counter and covered by a towel. Everyone who participated received a jar or two. During the next hour or two, we would hear the popping of the lids as the jars slowly cooled down. It was music to Georgia's ears and brought a smile to her face.

At one of those "unveiling of the crocks" parties, Georgia asked Jim, a third generation commercial fishing captain across the canal, "How much would it cost to take Joe out on your boat so he could learn some yellowtail snapper fishing." Jim replied, "It'll cost you one cheesecake." Georgia really made the best cheesecake and Jim loved it. Georgia said, "Done deal." We had another beautiful day out on the water as Mark and I learned a lot of techniques from Jim catching our fair share of yellowtails, with Georgia and Samantha along for the ride. When she had the restaurant, cheesecake was always on the menu, and she told us how she made an extra profit from a cake that came out of the oven with a big crack on the top of it. Because it wasn't presentable, it shouldn't be served as it is. It was expensive to make, and she didn't want to throw it out, so she covered it with chocolate, called it "Chocolate Cheesecake Supreme" and charged an extra fifty cents for it. Any time we were invited to a function, Georgia would ask, "What could we bring," and the response was always, "Cheesecake." Georgia even tried to get Linda to learn how to make it, giving her a spring pan and the recipe. Upon receiving them, Linda said, "I don't want to learn how to make cheesecake; it'll never taste as good as yours." To this day, I don't think she has.

Georgia also enjoyed making Irish Soda Bread once a year, usually a week or two before St. Patrick's Day, to give away as gifts to friends who really appreciated them. It was a time-consuming task a few years ago when she pumped out over three dozen of them. She would mail them to family in Arizona and friends in New York, but stopped after that last batch because of mailing costs. She then only made some to give away to local friends. Thinking back now, another sign of her not being up to par this past year—she didn't make any Irish Soda Bread for St. Patrick's Day.

We've also had sausage-making parties. We went to a local butcher to buy the skins, and ground up cheap cuts of pork in our own meat grinder. We usually let the women do the stuffing of the sausages as this drew much commentary from the male observers. We made hot and sweet Italian sausage and fresh kielbasa. We would do this a week or two before our Polish party where Ron and Mary would bring Ron's homemade pierogies and Ski and Betty would bring Betty's stuffed cabbage. We figured the Irish have St. Patrick's Day, the Italians have Columbus Day, so since I'm half Polish, we should also have a Polish Day celebration. We planned it around a week or two after St. Patrick's Day. Hey, it was another reason to party and have fun!

## CHAPTER IV

# Georgia, The Biker Chick

## HURRICANE JEAN

Initially, Georgia was not a biker chick. During our first marriage, I had a Harley sportster. She rode on it as a passenger one time from her house in Amityville to the restaurant—a distance of about seven miles. It was her only ride during that Joey II era. It limited my riding time because she wasn't into it. But during the Joey III era, that changed.

The year after we reconciled and were down in Florida, I told Georgia that I wanted to bring my bike down. I would have to fly up to New York and ride it down because I had no trailer at that time. She shocked me when she said she would like to take the ride down with me. The trip took us about a week because we planned on a few days stopover in Eatonton, Georgia. Our Florida Keys neighbors had a beautiful house on Lake Oconee. We spent a few leisurely days riding around on their pontoon boat and dining at a fine lakeside restaurant. On the day we left their lake house, we made it to the northern part of Florida where we stayed at a hotel. Listening to weather reports that night, they announced that Hurricane Jean was going to hit the East Coast of Florida between noon and 2:00 p.m. the next day. I went to the desk and tried to make a reservation to stay in that same hotel the next day, but it was already booked up. We were also told by the staff that the chance of getting a room anywhere south of there was highly unlikely.

We were on Interstate 75 heading south, so I told Georgia that if we left the hotel by 7:00 a.m., we just might miss it all together. I was thinking that if it hit the East Coast at that time, we could be south of it. That was quite a miscalculation! The morning started with cloudy skies, no rain, and very little wind. The clouds were drifting westerly and getting darker as the morning progressed. At around 10:00 a.m. a light rain started, but we kept going even as the rain and wind gradually increased. Eventually, the rain was coming down almost horizontally and at around noon, it took us two hours to go ten miles on the turnpike. We found out later that friends of ours, Donald and Joan, who were returning from The Villages heading home to their place in Summerland, had been on that stretch of the turnpike at the same time, saw us but didn't realize it was Georgia and me. They told us that they saw two bikers, one solo and one with a passenger, as that other biker accompanied us for a while during that stretch. I wish they had realized it was us so Georgia at least could have gotten into their car. If I had stayed on Interstate 75 rather than going onto the turnpike, chances would have been better that we could have missed most of the hurricane, but I thought we would make better time on the turnpike. We made it to Florida City at around 4:00 p.m. when it finally stopped raining and patches of blue sky started to appear—only one hundred miles to go to Big Pine Key. As we arrived home around 7:00 p.m. it was truly an endurance test, and Georgia passed it with flying colors as she never complained once.

## DROPPING THE BITCH

She accompanied me on several trips with friends I had made through Harley Owners Group (HOG), to various rallies and events. One particular one was the Vermont/New Hampshire Annual Rally. We went with a group of eleven bikers from our chapter—some solo, some with a passenger—riding on beautiful back roads with fantastic scenery. The group I was with liked the back roads rather than the interstates because not only the destination was enjoyable, but so was the journey.

On one day of riding, we came to a light at a four lane intersection from a two lane back road. Georgia and I were the sixth bike in the formation, and I caught a red light as the first five made it through. It was a long light because we were on a secondary road. When it finally changed, I made the left turn but couldn't see which way the first five bikers had gone because there was also a service road. Not initially seeing them on the main four lane road, I assumed they had taken the service road. As I was approaching the service road, I saw them way ahead on the main road. I made a sharp left, going only a few miles an hour, and started a right turn to get onto the main road just before a divider. I was doing less than five miles per hour, but I lost control on those almost ninety degree turns and dropped the bike with Georgia on the back. We didn't get hurt, but it was very embarrassing. I felt like that guy on *Laugh-In*, who rides his trike and just falls over. I had had rotator cuff surgery six weeks earlier, was doing physical therapy for it, and thought I had regained my full strength, but obviously I hadn't. The other bikers assisted me in uprighting the bike and we proceeded again. I only went a couple of feet more before I dropped the bike again. No one was hurt, except for my pride. It was very embarrassing. I guess between rotator cuff surgery and being a little top heavy with luggage on top of the tour pack, making a sharp turn at a slow speed made it difficult to maintain control. They say there are two kinds of riders—those who have fallen down, and those who never have, but someday will. I'm glad that neither of us got hurt and that I got that "someday will" out of the way, especially when doing such a slow speed.

## THE POSSE RUN

The following year I signed up for a cross country HOG-sponsored ride from Wilmington, Delaware to Portland, Oregon. It was called the "Posse Run." I signed up for it in January or February, and it was scheduled for July. Georgia wasn't going to go on this one and made plans with several girlfriends to spend some time in Atlantic City, Manhattan, and out at Montauk Point, Long Island. About two weeks before the ride, we were sitting on the couch watching TV when Georgia turned to me and asked if I would mind if she would go on this run with me. What a shock! I took out a saddle bag liner and told her that she could only take whatever would fit into that bag with her. I explained to her that some days we would be riding for a lot of hours racking up a lot of mileage. She said, "All right" and stated in the worst case scenario, I could drop her off at the nearest airport so she could fly back home. Mentally, I started plotting the airports for the first leg, from Islip MacArthur, JFK, and Newark to the Baltimore-Washington International Airport.

We traveled 9351 miles in thirty days and I didn't drop the "bitch" or the bike once. I say that lovingly and in reference to the tee-shirts some bikers wear that read on the back, "If you can read this, the bitch fell off." Georgia was a trooper. She has been on a lot of vacations and trips including Germany, Bermuda, Costa Rica, Greece, the Caribbean, Alaska, Hawaii, and later claimed that this adventure was the best vacation she had ever had. We started out with two other bikers, Eddie and Chet from our chapter, but Chet had to return home the first night because of medical problems in his family. Georgia made it, and we spent the first two nights in Wilmington.

On our first day out, we were almost run over by an eighteen-wheeler. We were just two bikes with Eddie in the lead position and we were in the left lane on an interstate highway in Pennsylvania (one of the few times we had done that). We were about one hundred feet behind a tractor-trailer. There was a slight drizzle and the roads were wet causing some backwash from the truck tires. There was another tractor-trailer in the right lane about six hundred feet ahead of the truck in the left lane. I guess this guy in the left lane was there to avoid getting the backwash from the truck in the right lane. We followed the left lane truck for a while anticipating that it would move over to the right lane. When it didn't, Eddie moved into the right lane and proceeded to pass it. I followed him but at a distance of one hundred feet so I would not get the backwash spray from his bike onto my windshield. When that trucker saw Eddie passing him on his right, he decided to move over into the right lane. Georgia and I were alongside him when he started to pull over into our lane. I assume he never saw us, probably because of that backwash, as I saw this massive white trailer getting closer and closer. Because the roads were wet and I was going at a faster rate of speed than he was, I didn't apply my brakes. Instead, I increased my speed and rode on the shoulder as he occupied the whole right lane. I finally passed him and reentered the right lane. I hope he wound up with a brown spot in his underwear as he sure as hell scared the crap out of us. People have often asked, "What do you do when it rains?" We replied, "We get wet." Well, that was a wet one, but we survived. While the weather was mostly good, the temperature did reach one hundred eight degrees on one day, and dove into the low forties on another day. It's all part of the experience.

Riding a bike cross country gives you a chance to really enjoy the scenery as you feel, breathe, and absorb this great country. The corn belt seems to have doubled in the last few years, probably because of the ethanol added to our gas, for we rode day after day seeing nothing but cornfields, and not just in Iowa. The Great Plains seemed to go on forever, the mountains are magnificent, the forests are beautiful, and the vastness of this land is overwhelming. "From sea to shining sea" is just a phrase in the song "America the Beautiful," but traveling from one coast to the other is an experience of a lifetime, especially on a bike. I've had the opportunity of doing it once in a motor home and twice on a bike, but this time with Georgia.

Still heading west, while riding on some back roads in Montana, with nothing but miles and miles of rolling prairie and hardly any trees on either side, we would come upon a single house in the middle of nowhere. There were no other buildings, structures, dwellings, or visible human habitation nor were there any animals for ten or fifteen miles in either direction of it. Georgia asked me, "What would make a person decide to build a house right there?" There was no cultivated land by the house and the nearest neighbor had to be fifteen minutes away. We assumed they liked their solitude. That particular day was also a stiflingly hot one. There was only a slight breeze under a clear blue sky with a

*In beautiful Montana*

*One of the cold days*

sizzling sun beating down on us. As we rode through a small town about one hour later, we saw a reading of one hundred eight degrees on a bank time/temperature sign. While riding, you don't feel it as much, but when slowing down or stopping, you do. After gassing up the bikes and quenching our thirst, we put on our AC's (opened the vents on the front lower fairings and the deflectors on the upper ones) and continued riding so we could cool off.

Prior to our leaving on this trip, Georgia suggested that I call Rosemarie, a woman I had met on a previous HOG event named the "Lewis and Clark Run." That event also ended in Seaside, Oregon, where Rosemarie lived. I was solo on that one and as I pulled into a designated area just for bikers, I heard Rosemarie state she had never been on a motorcycle, and it was on her bucket list to do. I told her to hop on and I would take her for a ride. Originally she said no; she would have to ask her husband first. I told her to go ask him and she said, "The heck with asking him," and added, "Let's go." A photographer and a reporter were there and took our picture as we rode off. When we returned after a short ride, I was interviewed and they took another picture. I gave Rosemarie a token good luck coin that HOG had given us to hand out to people we would meet along the way, in the spirit of the Lewis and Clark Expedition. She said she wanted to give me a loaf of her butternut cake. I told her I had no room on the bike, but if she wanted, she could send me one at Christmas instead, and she agreed. A week before Christmas, a package arrived with her cake, some cookies, and an article I was totally unaware of from their local newspaper, the Daily Astorian. In it was a photo of me displaying my Lewis and Clark log which was signed by Nancy and Willie G. Davidson (grandson of one of the founders of Harley Davidson motorcycles). Willie G. had given up going to Sturgis that year (which he had done every year for the last twenty or so years) so that he could be part of this experience. On the back page was a picture of Rosemarie and me as we pulled out of the parking lot with her wearing a great big smile. Rosemarie and I exchanged Christmas cards in the ensuing years.

I called Rosemarie a week before we were to leave and arranged to meet her and her husband, Don, on the day we would be in Seaside. It was a brief conversation and Georgia asked to speak to her. Rosemarie confided

*Rosemary Schenk, visiting Seaside from Tigard, laughs as she takes a ride on the back of Joe McKasty's Harley-Davidson. "I was bold enough to ask and the gentleman was nice enough to say yes," says Schenk, who was tickled by her ride down Broadway. (Photo courtesy of The Daily Astorian, Oregon, August 9, 2002.)*

to Georgia that she lost her Lewis and Clark good luck coin the previous year and had ailments, dental problems, and bad luck with some members in her family, but she didn't want to tell me. Georgia told me afterwards, and I just happened to have three coins left from that trip. Now years later on this Posse Run, we were also given good luck trinkets to pass out to people we would meet along the way. About three weeks after talking with Rosemarie, we hooked up again with her and Don in our hotel dining room. This presented another video moment as Eddie recorded me presenting Don rather than Rosemarie with a Posse Run Good Luck Coin since she kept losing them. But then, after a slight pause, I pulled out a Lewis and Clark Coin to present to her and you would have thought I had given her a thousand dollar prize. Now why did she not tell me that she lost the original coin? Georgia had never even met her, and she confided in Georgia instead of me.

The next day we went south to Redway in Northern California. Georgia's Aunt Bea, who had no children of her own and treated Georgia like a daughter, had a goddaughter named Sandy who lived there. Georgia and Sandy had had infrequent contact throughout the years, but had never met. Georgia called prior to leaving on this trip and Sandy had invited us to stay at her place when we got out there. We arranged to meet at some local landmark a few miles from her home so that she could escort us to it. When we had spoken before the trip, she asked me if we minded riding on a dry riverbed. I told her that would not be a problem, and we met her and her boyfriend—both on their own bikes as well. They then led the way. We went a few miles and the road went from blacktop to gravel to dirt. Then we got to the riverbed. It was about five hundred feet wide with dry river stone in the middle and two small one lane bridges on either side, each just fifty to one hundred feet long, with no guardrail on either one and rutted river stone on both. The bridges were only a few feet above the river which was very low at this time of year. Sandy told us later that during the wet season, both bridges are under water and that's why they have river stone on them. They then have to travel thirty extra miles to get from her place to town. Because we were traveling so slowly and it was rutted and bumpy, I envisioned the possibility of us falling over the edge into the very shallow river. I kept repeating to myself, "Not gonna drop the bike and her, not gonna drop her." We finally got across the first one, and we were then in the middle of the dry riverbed. It was a lot easier and as we approached the far side bridge, I knew what to expect which made it easier to cross as we finally made it to the other bank.

It was an all dirt and gravel road the rest of the way to Sandy's place, which was the very last house on the road. There was an unused railroad track line on the left side of the road, with a lumber company's miles of undeveloped acreage on the other side of it. We passed very few houses before getting to hers, which had a great view of the river and was about a quarter mile from it. Eddie really enjoyed our stay there as he rode their dune buggy on the dry riverbed and got in some target practice with his pistol. We all also enjoyed pears, apples, and berries from their orchard. They truly were gracious hosts. Crossing over that riverbed when we left was easier now because we knew what to expect. It was another fantastic episode on this adventurous journey all because Georgia wanted to meet her Aunt Bea's goddaughter.

Leaving there, we rode through several national parks as we headed to Reno, Nevada. Northern California is beautiful country to ride in. Actually seeing those Giant Redwoods and standing beside them makes you realize how truly magnificent they are. We stayed two nights in Reno giving us and the bikes one full day to rest, and providing opportunity to make a donation in various casinos. Then we headed north to Coeur D'Alene, Idaho. We minimized traveling on interstate routes and took secondary roads as often as we could, and it took us two days to get there. I tried to hook up with my grandkids, Coralynn and Quinn, but that didn't happen because of visitation problems between my son Michael and his ex-wife. We had ridden hundreds of miles up there basically to see them. My son rode all the way from Long Island, New York for a court date and visitation, and his ex-wife and new husband kept hiding the kids from him. So I told his ex-wife that because she would not allow my son his entitled joint custody visitation rights, I would therefore not visit the kids in the hope she would reconsider. She didn't acknowledge my son's rights and the fact that we didn't see the kids was the only downside of this whole trip. I never did get to see or speak to Quinn again because he died years later in a car accident.

After that disappointment, we started heading out eastward, but when we made a pit stop at around 2:00 p.m., we were informed about the lack of availability of hotel rooms. Wild fires were forcing campers to vacate the parks and go to the hotels and motels. So we decided to head back to Spokane, Washington where we had stayed the night before, but nothing was available there either because of boat races, ball tournaments, and numerous other events all going on at the same time. We headed east again and stopped at every hotel/motel with the same result—no vacancy. We went through Coeur D'Alene and then decided to head north again stopping at each hotel finding nothing available. Just before the Canadian Border we turned east and went into Montana. It was about an hour before sunset and we still had no hotel to check in to. We were on a two lane road in a very sparsely populated area and we were getting a little concerned.

Finally Eddie spotted a very small highway sign for an Amber Bear Inn with an arrow pointing to the right. He radioed me and asked if we should try it because it was off our route. I told him it was worth a shot at this late hour. We followed the signage for the Inn and became more concerned as the narrow road turned to a gravel and dirt road with hardly any houses on either side. Now it was starting to get dark. We commented how this would be a perfect setting for a Stephen King novel when the road ended at this great big upwardly sloping open field with a good-sized building straight ahead at the far end and a big mountain behind it. It was a perfect setting for one of his novels! The building was a six room inn and restaurant with a barn and cabin to the left. We parked our bikes, went inside and got the same response—no vacancy at the Inn, but a little cabin was available for the night for $100. We didn't want to seem overanxious so we said we'd have to check it out. We would have paid triple that, especially after trying to get a room at over twenty places for the last six or seven hours. It only had a queen bed, but Ed said he'd have no problem sleeping on the floor. This place was like an oasis to us. The Inn's restaurant was closed because the chef had just left prior to our arrival, but the owner's wife, Nancy, fixed us a fantastic meal; I don't remember what it was, but the complimentary wine enhanced it, and this stay wound up being another highlight of our trip.

I awoke around 6:00 a.m. the next day to the sight of a head strutting past our window. I had to get up to see what the heck that was all about. Looking out the window, I saw a llama just meandering about. I woke Georgia and we went outside, and saw the llama grazing in the field, with a beautiful view of a lake to our right and a herd of roaming elk. The big open field had to be ten to fifteen acres with some deer to the left and a horse, peacocks, goats, and guinea hens scattered here and there. Georgia stated that she felt like we had gone from a Stephen King setting to a Walt Disney scene. There were little doghouse-like chicken coops where we were invited to lift up the roofs and pick as many eggs as we wanted for breakfast. We then brought them to the chef, told him how we wanted them cooked, and were then served a fantastic breakfast.

When we finished, Mike the owner took us on a tour of part of the property in his four seat golf cart. After visiting the animals in the barn, we went on a trail up to the top of the mountain. He said someone would have to get out and push the cart in a few spots where the incline was a little too steep for a fully loaded cart to make the climb. Poor Eddie got stuck a few times doing the pushing because I was busy doing the videotaping. When we reached the top, it was a breathtaking view of all those sites; the Inn, the field, the lake, and the other mountains. It was a magnificent view of Montana country where everything is clear, crisp, green, and sunny. The Amber Bear Inn experience was another of the highlights on that "Posse Run" ride.

Later that morning we hit the road heading east on Route 2. It was a perfect day—the scenery, the weather, the people, and the ride. Unfortunately, we saw smoke several times from various forest fires that were still burning. We made it to Eastern Montana by the end of the day and were lucky enough to get a room on our fourth or fifth try. When we left the motel the next morning we only rode twenty-five miles when we encountered a problem. We were in a thirty or forty miles per hour zone most of the time because of residential and industrial areas until we finally got to a fifty-five mile per hour zone. It had to be frustrating for Eddie because he likes open roads and maximum speeds. He was on the left side of the left lane with me behind him on the right side of that left lane when, instead of accelerating as I had expected him to do, he started slowing down and pulling to the right. I wondered, what was the matter with him, and then noticed the back of his bike waddling side to side as he continued to the shoulder of the road. Just before he came to a stop, the bike fell to the right, dumping Eddie onto an open field. He was all right, but the bike had a flat tire. We both had our rear tires replaced just before the start of this trip and there was still plenty of tread on both of them.

Eddie called for a tow truck to take the bike to the nearest Harley Dealer. Knowing the scarcity of available rooms, he suggested that I go back to the motel we had just left and get some rooms again. I agreed, and Georgia hopped on the back of the bike. I was about to take off when he stopped me saying, "You ain't going anywhere, your tire is going flat too." Now we were wondering how the two of us could have gotten flat tires when they were both brand new ones. Then we remembered that on the previous day we had ridden on a three to four mile stretch of road that was being repaired with newly mined sharp gravel on it. We figured that the sharp gravel had to be the cause of our flat tires. But Eddie (who should have been nicknamed "MacGyver" after that TV character who could get out of any predicament) had a solution. He fitted an inflation device onto a Co2 cartridge that he always carried on the bike and inflated my tire using three cartridges. It would not have worked on his bike because the bead was broken on his tire. I then went without Georgia to reserve our rooms, stopping at the first gas station to further inflate the tire. Because it was a Sunday, the Harley Dealer was closed and we had to stay another night in that area.

After both our tires were replaced the next day, we continued on our journey. There were no more incidents for the rest of the trip as we visited more parks, local attractions, and enjoyed the ride. Where we stopped was a blur because the ride now became the experience. From having ridden on a bike only once during our first marriage, Georgia truly became a biker chick on this run, with 9351 miles to her credit. After that Posse Ride I felt like John Travolta in *Grease* when Olivia Newton-John transformed from a socialite into a "greaser." Enduring all those cross-country miles on the back of a motorcycle in all kinds of conditions transformed Georgia into that biker chick. In later years, she repeatedly related how this adventure was the greatest vacation experience she had ever had, and she did accompany me on a few more Upstate runs in later years.

## TRAILERING THE BIKE

When Georgia and I left the Keys, we always timed our northbound trailering trips back to Long Island to arrive before Memorial Day. Besides honoring our military, Onkel's family of Klapproths, Lunts, and Marinos always hosted a picnic at Southaven Park for family, extended family, and friends. Naturally, Georgia and I were always invited and there always was a softball game consisting of players aged pre-school to their seventies. It was more of a fun game rather than a competitive one, and one year I was awarded the game ball, but not because of my athletic ability. I was the losing pitcher, never got a hit, and needed a base runner if I did. I believe I received it because of Onk's family's love and respect for Georgia and her devotion to him. It also helped that I had on an Onkel Herman's Softball Team shirt that Georgia had given me to wear that had to be at least forty years old.

Georgia loved the need for me to have to trailer my bike between New York and Florida. Besides the room in the back seat of the crew cab and the covered bed of the pickup, towing an enclosed bike trailer provided a lot more cargo space for her to bring some of her goodies to both locations. Besides strapping a forty-two inch Curious George monkey to the bike, she had room to transport potted starter plants up north along with yard sale treasures she purchased as gifts for others. When we headed south, it was to save potted hot pepper plants that would have died had she not taken them. Again, there were also yard sale items, cartons, and objects belonging to her friends that she volunteered to haul either way for them because they had no room in their vehicles when they traveled north or south. And there were always a few boxes and bags of stuffed and animated monkeys for her entourage. On the last trip up to New York, I had to position and secure the bike to a side slot to allow enough room for a provincial style monkey fabric upholstered chair to be loaded on. She never drove any of those 1500 miles in either direction, but she was grateful for that extra cargo space in the trailer. Naturally, going in either direction we had to stop in Inverness, Florida to see her Uncle John and Aunt Mary and her cousins Chris, Maryann, Jamie, and Marissa.

## ROCK, RHYTHM, AND BLUES

She participated in her last long HOG Run in 2011—"The Rock, Rhythm, and Blues Tour." Normally, Georgia and I trailered my bike up from Florida to New York in May, but this time we dropped it off at Eddie's house in Port St. Lucie, Florida. I then flew down to Florida, and Eddie and I rode our bikes to New Orleans, where the tour started. Georgia flew there and joined us. She enjoyed listening to her music and really enjoyed the multitude of sounds on this tour starting with the jazz and blues of New Orleans and ending with rock 'n' roll in Cleveland, Ohio. We spent three days in New Orleans and on our first day out, we stopped in Meridian, Mississippi to see the Jimmie Rodgers Museum honoring the "Father of Country Music." Next, we went to Memphis, Tennessee and toured Graceland, Elvis Presley's home, then on to the Grand Ole Opry in Nashville where we saw stage performances by Carrie Underwood, Lady Antebellum,

Martina McBride, Darius Rucker, and the Oak Ridge Boys. It just happened to be Country Awards Week and we lucked out by seeing an awesome show. The "Rock, Rhythm, and Blues Tour" ended with a tour at the Rock and Roll Hall of Fame with all of those events included in our package at no extra cost.

Because Eddie had other plans, I left Cleveland around 7:00 a.m. with another biker and I told Georgia, who was flying back, that I would see her sometime the next day expecting to take two days to reach Manorville, Long Island. She arranged for transportation to the airport and expected to arrive back home around 6:00 p.m. The other biker and I made such good time that we rode non-stop, and I arrived home at around 5:30 p.m. that same day. I parked the bike in the garage, closed the overhead door, and kept the front door locked. I poured myself a wine, sat in my recliner, and waited for Georgia to walk through the front door. When she finally got home and came through the front door, I asked her if she would like a cocktail. She cursed me out for scaring the heck out of her, but got over it very quickly as we had our cocktails and reminisced about another great adventure we had both just shared.

*On Whiteface Mountain*

# CHAPTER

V

# The Hospital Stays

**D**amn it. Another medical warning sign was that she never got into her gardening this year, neither in the Keys nor up north. Both gardens had to be fenced in because of foraging deer in both locations. She planted Big Boy and Cherry tomatoes, eggplants, and herbs, but mostly bell and hot peppers. Besides her jalapeños and habaneros, she grew various other ones, even some from seeds that my brother, Kevin, sent from Alaska. She grew them to make hot pepper jelly to give away to those brave enough to withstand the heat, like Linda and Christy at the No Name Pub. From November of last year to when we left the Keys to go back up north in May, she only occasionally got into her garden. She asked me to take the fence down as she didn't have the energy to do it anymore. When we headed north we brought three tomato plants and four pepper plants with us that she had started from seed. We brought two parsley plants later after getting up north and that was the extent of her north garden this year. I planted the tomato and pepper plants as soon as we got there and placed the two parsley plants in their pots on the ground expecting she would get around to planting them. She never did.

## THE BEST BARS OF NEW YORK

Some years back, Sue, our next door neighbor in Manorville, gave Georgia a hardcover book entitled, *The History and Stories of the Bars of New York*. It gave her a new objective in her retirement years, which she did not get to achieve. She wanted to visit each one of the bars, and get an owner or manager of those she visited to sign the corresponding page in the book, but unfortunately she only got to visit six out of the thirty listed. She was a city girl, having lived in the Al Smith Projects in lower Manhattan by the Brooklyn Bridge until she married Joe I. There were some blank pages in the book that she used for three of her favorite bars not listed, like the Holiday Bar where her mother tended bar for many years, or El Faro's which she frequented in her early years. The Wurlitzer Jukebox her mother bought for her from the Holiday Bar is now downstairs and still plays her 45 rpm records. Georgia enjoyed telling the story of how "Lefty Guns" of Donnie Brasco fame had paid for her sister's prom dress since they were frequent customers at the Holiday Bar.

## THE TIMES IN A HOSPITAL

In early June, she finally agreed to go see a doctor. She was referred by my doctor to see a gastroenterologist who sent her to Brookhaven Hospital for testing. She was hurting as her abdomen was swelling and she had to be admitted ten days later. She wouldn't let anyone know the pain she was in, or the difficulty she had getting around or moving about. She was in the hospital five days and they drained four liters of fluid from her abdomen. On Wednesday of the following week she had a follow-up appointment with her doctor who she claimed punched her in the stomach a few times. She was still hurting after all they had done so far, and even more so now. That night, her stomach started leaking a clear liquid from the spot where they had gone in to do the procedure. You couldn't even tell where they went in and that leaking spot just looked like perspiration. I called her doctor the next day to voice our concern and my desire to get her back to the hospital, but he said not to, as the Fourth of July weekend was coming up and not much would be done anyway. He advised that she sleep with that leaky side up and she would be all right. The next morning, the Fourth of July, both sheets were soaking wet because of the leakage. I said to myself, "It's time for a new doctor and a new hospital." It took another day to convince her to go again to the hospital.

On July fifth, I took her to Stony Brook Hospital. Being directionally challenged, it took a while for her to realize we were not heading in the direction of the other hospital and she questioned why. I told her when we left the house that we were going to Stony Brook, but I guess she didn't hear me. I then told her I wasn't happy with the treatment she was getting from her doctor, and because Stony Brook was a university hospital, treatment should be better there. She was unhappy at first, and I told her I would turn around if she wanted, but she finally agreed to go there. This time it was a three day stay as they drained about two more liters of fluid from her. They did that in the Emergency Room, and Georgia was again in a lot of pain during that two hour procedure. I found out later that the First of July is when new people start, and it looked like she had to endure someone practicing on her. Also, it had always been difficult to have needles put into her veins for blood work and intravenous hookups. Again, it seemed like there were more people practicing on her as it took over a dozen attempts to locate and/or penetrate her veins.

She was released on July seventh and had a severe case of diarrhea the next few days. She couldn't walk without assistance, could not walk up the stairs, did not eat, and slept in the downstairs bedroom. I bought a folding commode and placed it next to her bed. She refused to go back to the hospital until Saturday the twelfth. A day or two later they informed us she had an infection called C.diff, short for Clostridium difficile. She got it from taking antibiotics during the previous hospital stay. Those antibiotics kill most bacteria, but C.diff survives, reproducing in large numbers and secretes a toxin causing diarrhea. The medical staff then had to try to find the right balance of probiotics and antibiotics to administer to her. The probiotics they gave her were in a small packet put on her food tray. She didn't know it was her medication and thinking it was a towel wipe, did not take it the first day. The first attempt to take it the next day didn't go too well either as it was in a powdered form and had to be mixed with liquid. The next attempt was to mix it in applesauce, with the same result—she just couldn't swallow it. Meanwhile, she was in constant pain with cramps from suppressing the urge to go, and she was being denied any pain medication because of the antibiotics. Every time she felt as though she had to go, which was frequent, she would attempt to suppress it crying, "No, no, not again." During those first few days, she was escorted by a nurse or an aide to the bathroom. So I guess they gave her the medication intravenously and she started to improve so much so, that they said she could be released in another day or two to a rehabilitation center to start exercising muscles to get her walking again. It became more convenient for Georgia, and the staff, to have her use a folding commode right alongside her bed in the latter part of the week. They gave me a five page list of several rehabilitation centers and representatives from four came to her room, gave us brochures, and informed us of their services. That week was like a roller coaster ride with many ups and downs in her progress. It looked very promising, but she couldn't be released until the infection was gone. Because she still had the infection, they now told us she was not ready for rehabilitation and had to stay in the hospital over the weekend.

The following week was also another up and down emotional ride. At the beginning of the week, the staff again informed us she should be ready in a day or two to go to a rehabilitation facility. Again, another representative from one of the centers gave us a brochure, and we were planning on a release from the hospital once more. But she was still constantly hurting. It was difficult for any hospital worker to draw blood from her. She said on one occasion when I wasn't there, that eighteen attempts were made to hook her up to an intravenous needle, which had to be changed every four days. Eventually they had to hook one up into her neck as they had no success attempting to put one into either arm. Because she had so much trouble breathing, she was now on oxygen with those two little tubes going up her nostrils.

## GERMAN ROOMMATE

On Wednesday, Debbie, a former waitress and one of her best friends, paid Georgia a visit wearing her dirndl. Georgia had gotten a new roommate, Annie, a few days earlier. As soon as Annie started talking, Georgia heard a German accent. It brightened her up as she related the news about Annie to Debbie, and it prompted Debbie to volunteer to wear the dirndl on her next visit. Georgia and Annie had a lot to talk about, as Annie and her husband had both been to the restaurant and to the same places in Germany that Georgia visited. I had to bring three photo albums recording our trips to Germany, along with two quarts of our homemade sauerkraut to give to Annie. We had just made that batch before we came up north. Annie had her daughter take a picture on her cell phone of Georgia and Debbie. Later that afternoon, Debbie called me, as I was having brakes replaced on my truck, to inform me that Georgia had just aspirated. When I got there, she could communicate, but it was an effort for her.

Georgia stated she was not going to leave the hospital alive this time.

Again, I didn't want to hear that. She improved slightly the next two days, but on Friday she relapsed. Now a realization set in. She's NOT getting better. She can't be right. I went down to the Patient Advocate Office. No other clients were there as I went directly to the girl behind the counter. She asked if she could help me. I couldn't speak. She could see I was hurting. I shook my head no when she asked me if I wanted a glass of water or asked if I wanted to sit down. Every time I was about to say something, I choked up. It took about four or five minutes before I could say, "She's not getting any better," and then I started crying. It took another few minutes for me to calm down enough to give her Georgia's name. I then proceeded to tell her what had transpired in the last two weeks resulting in Georgia's lack of progress.

When I went back to Georgia's room, she was wearing a full oxygen mask, had a tube down her throat, and was hooked up to eight intravenous bottles. She looked tired, pale, and weak. She could only speak a few words at a time, and she could hardly move. The roller coaster ride was now all downhill. I felt so helpless seeing her condition worsen and knowing there was nothing I could do to make her better. It really hurts to see your loved one in a situation where you are powerless to help. All I could do was put on a brave front and tell her positive things about her getting better, pulling through this, going to rehab, and coming home.

They moved her to the fourteenth floor that night and then to the seventeenth floor after that. I don't know if it was a result of my seeing the Patient Advocate or just a normal procedure because of her condition, but we were both happier as her care improved greatly. Unfortunately her condition did not. Those last three days were a heartbreaker.

On Saturday she could only minimally communicate because of the oxygen mask and her shortness of breath. It was a major effort for her to speak a few words and she was hooked up to eight intravenous bottles. It was easier for her to write a word or two for me than for me to interpret what she was trying to say. On Sunday our communication was me asking questions and she responding with yes or no head nods. I'd been averaging five to six hours a day with her in the hospital all this time and Monday was the toughest day. I got there around 9:00 a.m. and had been sitting with her for two to three hours, but she was mostly in an unconscious state. Every once in a while though, she would nod a little monkey that she constantly held in her hand, and I at that time, thought she was indicating a hello. Thinking back, I now know she was saying goodbye.

## MAKING THE DECISION

At around 1:00 p.m., a large group of medical personnel came in and told me to leave her room so they could evaluate her. One came back out twenty minutes later to inform me that she had to go on life support with a ventilator and a dialysis machine, and they wanted my permission. I immediately told them yes. As they were organizing the implementation of those procedures, I was given some forms to sign and again asked if that was what I wanted and if this is what Georgia would have wanted. Georgia and I had discussed this before, and in 2005 we both signed a durable power of attorney for healthcare. In it she declared she did not want antibiotics, blood transfusions, or mechanical respiration. She already was on antibiotics and had blood transfusions, but there was no way she would have wanted to be hooked up to a respirator or a dialysis machine. Knowing this, I asked how long she would survive without them. They said it could be hours or a day or two. Now I had to make "THE" decision. Smack! Wham! Oh My God! They told me to sit down as I lost it again and the tears started flowing. I knew what she wanted, but to tell them not to hook her up meant I was allowing her to die. When you sign those healthcare proxies, you don't think about when the time may come when you'll have to fulfill those directives. I thought if anything, she would have to make that decision for me as I was older. Even though I knew this was what she wanted, I was reluctant to tell them not to hook her up. It was difficult, but because it was a decision she had made, I told them not to put her on life support, and then I lost it again.

I made contact with her two girlfriends, Dale and Debbie, (I don't remember if I called them or if they called me) and told them about the situation. They showed up at around 3:00 or 4:00 p.m. and were there as Georgia passed away at 5:52 p.m. on July twenty-eighth. And the tears started flowing again for us and for many of the people she knew as they were informed. Almost all were in shock. All this time when she had been in the hospital, and even before, she avoided answering her phone and returning calls. Before she went in, she told very few people about her ailments or how she really felt. She didn't want the attention, to hear people telling her to see a doctor, or that she should get some testing done.

## GEORGIA
### January 24, 1947 – July 28, 2014

*Weep not is what I'm trying to say. Live your life to the fullest day by day. Give of yourself to your fellow man. Offer whatever you have and extend your hand. This is what I have tried to do. Now, I am saying this to you; remember me in your daily prayers. For I was there for you and I really cared. I loved you and you showed me love back. I will never forget you and never forget me.*

---

**LINDENHURST FUNERAL HOME**
631-957-0300

## CHAPTER

# VI

# Saying Goodbye

## THE ARRANGEMENTS

We met John, the Funeral Director on Tuesday afternoon, to make the arrangements. I, Georgia's nephew, his girlfriend, his son, and my son were there. After I gave John her name and some information about the family, he asked for information about her. When I informed him she owned Georgia's German Restaurant, he was surprised. He exclaimed, "This is Georgia?" He didn't know Georgia, as very, very few people did, by her full name of Georgette Calogeras McKasty, and I was the only person who called her Georgette. After I gave him some information about her party-making days, I requested she be listed in the obituary section under Georgia only. Because, just like him, nobody would recognize her if she was not. He agreed.

Upon receiving the next day's edition of Newsday, our local newspaper, I noticed she was not listed as Georgia in the obituary section. I called the Newsday Obituary Department and spoke to a woman who said they could not honor my request. They just don't do first name only listings. I told her nobody was going to know it was Georgia by that full name listing, as they only know her as "Georgia." She told me people would realize it was her when they read the whole listing. I told her all the people I know just look at the names for people they recognize. If they don't recognize the name, they don't read what's written about people they don't know, and they proceed to scan the rest of the names. I hung up the phone in anger when she said she couldn't do it. I then called John at the funeral home and informed him of my conversation with Newsday. I reminded him of how he didn't know it was Georgia under her full legal name. He said he would look into it, and the next day's obituary had her listed as Georgia. Thank you, John.

John also had asked me to bring in some photos of Georgia to put on display boards. Between New York and Florida, we had over three dozen photo albums and several boxes of photos from the last few years that hadn't yet made it into more albums. I told him it would be impossible to select some, and instead brought seventeen of the twenty plus albums we had up north to her wake for everyone to see how much fun she had and they were spread all around the room among her monkeys. Her relatives took four from her early days back home, as they were more meaningful to them.

## SHIPPING THE MONKEYS

On that Tuesday morning I called Linda, another best girlfriend down in the Keys, to ask for a major favor. I requested that she ship all of Georgia's stuffed monkeys to me so they could be on Long Island for her wake. She enlisted the help of my Florida Keys next door neighbors, Mark and Samantha, to pack them into three of FedEx's biggest boxes. I asked them to overnight the packages no matter how much it cost. They did and on the following first day of a two day wake, the truck arrived at around 10:00 a.m. There was only one package delivered so I asked about the other two, but the driver said that was all he had. It cost almost $400 to ship each box overnight. I would have gladly paid that, but two of the three boxes didn't arrive until the following day, so instead of paying $1200 for those deliveries, Mark and Samantha obtained a refund of $800. There were over one hundred monkeys in those boxes. Because these monkeys were such a vital part of her life, I felt they had to be there. She knew who gave her each one and had names for most of them. I also wanted each person who came to the wake to take one home as a remembrance of Georgia. Those that were shipped plus the ones she already had up north amounted to almost two hundred monkeys in all.

Annie, her last hospital roommate, printed that picture she took of Georgia and Debbie and put it into a frame. One day after she got out of the hospital, she showed up at the wake with her daughter and gave Debbie that last picture of the two of them together. Then, Debbie gave it to me. It just goes to show the affect Georgia had on people, as Annie had only met her less than two weeks ago. Stephen, her bartender who chauffeured us to our first date, told others at the wake how indebted he was to Georgia. His first bartending job was at Georgia's. At that time he lived in Astoria and had to commute by train to Lindenhurst, Long Island, and then taxi or walk over a mile to her restaurant. He would show up punctually every day, even during snow storms when one of her staff who lived locally, couldn't make it in. He is now part owner of a very successful restaurant, the Irish Coffee Pub, Islip, Long Island, New York. He had expressed his gratitude to Georgia many times, and she was proud of his success.

## MILLIE'S DAUGHTERS

Millie, the lady I lived with for four and a half years before Georgia, had four daughters I had minimal contact with after Millie's death in 1983. Linda, the second oldest and I maintained annual contact, meeting at a restaurant usually just before Georgia and I headed back down south. In fact, it became a standard comment from Georgia every time we passed Tang's Chinese Restaurant when we came to Lindenhurst that it was time to give Linda a call. Kelly, the youngest, was just a teenager when her mother and I were together.

At that time, Kelly and I did not get along. I guess

I was an imagined competition for her mother's attention or some teenage girl issues got in the way because we had an abrasive relationship. However, all the girls, and Millie's father, did come to our wedding in 1991. After the wedding, contact was very minimal and wound up being mostly with Linda. When she came to the wake in the afternoon and updated me about her sisters, I was shocked to learn that Kelly had five kids and was also a grandmother—Kelly, the "Brat," a grandmother! Unbelievable!

That night, all four of Millie's daughters came to the wake—Georgia, Linda, Donna, and Kelly. Kelly and I now email each other and she refers to herself as the "Brat." Thinking back to when Millie and I were together, I remembered when Millie's father, Pasquale, would call Millie, "Brat." Georgia loved Pasquale, in spite of his old Italian ways, and we visited him quite often because he lived right around the corner from the restaurant. We were glad they all came to our wedding in 1991, and I'm thankful all the girls came to Georgia's wake.

## THE EULOGY

Besides assisting with the packing of the stuffed monkeys

to send up north, Linda, from Big Pine Key, also flew up for the wake. I couldn't accommodate anyone else in my condo, so Sue, my next door neighbor, was gracious enough to put her up. Linda, one of Georgia's several best friends, was like a sister to her.

At Georgia's service on Friday, I asked an old friend of mine, Reverend Phil, to officiate the liturgy, as neither Georgia nor I were church goers. He did a decent job for not knowing her, but he thought she was German because she owned a German Restaurant. I had to correct him during his presentation and tell him she was of Greek-Irish descent.

He then told everyone there not to forget me during this difficult time—to bring over food, not realizing how overfull my refrigerator was as a result of people already doing that. He then asked if anyone wanted to say something about Georgia. Linda asked if she could come to the front of the room to say something. He invited her up and she gave a eulogy for about ten minutes that spoke from the heart. I don't remember much of what she said other than how much Georgia had touched her and the hearts of all those she had befriended. She touched Linda's heart enough for her to come all the way up from Florida. Thank you, Linda.

During this past summer before Georgia went into the hospital, Linda asked her if she could obtain a Yuengling beer tap handle for Ray, Linda's husband. It took a while, but Mike, who went to Germany with us, had an extra one to give to her. It made Georgia feel good to know that she could fulfill that request because of the friendship she still had with other restaurant owners.

# People Remember

A week or so after the wake, in a condolence card from Frank and Patty, the honeymooning couple Georgia and I met on our first date on that cruise, Patty stated:

> *We've been thinking about you both of late. When we didn't get our annual Christmas card, we were worried. It wasn't like her not to stay in touch. No matter how she passed, we hope she didn't suffer. We will always keep our fond memories of her close in our hearts and we wish you peace as you heal.*

And Just before Thanksgiving, Jane, another best friend, sent her condolence card. The card said:

*Through everything you shared together—
the years you loved each other, the warmth
and caring between you—you created a
special bond that will always be a part of
you…Hoping you find now in that very
special love—a love that will last forever.*

Then she wrote in the card:

*While card shopping, I believe Georgia led
me to this one. I feel her presence often.
Upon my return to Kismet this summer,
I walked into the Inn and "Would You be
My Girl" was playing. Your sweet Maimou
is so missed. Our love and thoughts are
with you.*

Then included in the card was this note. It read:

*Dear Joe, I found this card some time
ago, it seemed so appropriate for you.
Yet I couldn't bring myself to send it until
now. As Thanksgiving approaches, you
have been in our thoughts and each time
I have felt saddened by the loss of Georgia,
I try to think of one of the many happy
and wonderful memories we shared.
I realize that no matter the season or
place, I have a "Georgia memory!" This
fall has been especially so, because I*

*kept anticipating a call for a quick get-together before heading south. Or that she was getting the "gang together at the old place." Going back further, I think of the two of us in our "getting fit" mode, walking the neighborhood as Halloween decorations became Christmas lights and she told me her amazing story of secretly making chocolate and selling it to become independent. Then working for Onkel Herman and her signature moxie and hard work, transforming her place into the successful, iconic "Georgia's German Restaurant." Memories of the many adventures that you and she, Louie, and I shared are forever tucked into my heart.*

She continued:

*One of the most touching is of Georgia transforming her office into a nursery and then, picturing her face the moment she met Nicholas (Jane's son) and witnessing the powerful bond immediately forged between the two. Nick has been particularly touched by our loss of Georgia. He keeps her remembrance card on his wall, a daily reminder to follow the message of her essence. As much as we miss her, I cannot even imagine how quiet your world has gotten; you made one of those rare and wonderful couples who bring out the very best in the other. As you have said, "Nobody had more fun than Georgia!" Lest we never forget—"The Queen of the Dead Flies!" With much love, Jane.*

"The Queen of the Dead Flies" statement is in reference to a day on our boat when Jane was helping us winterize it during our first marriage. As Jane and I were doing some of the unpacking, draining, and cleaning, Georgia decided to rest because of having so much fun the night before, on the booth in the galley, which had quite a few big dead green horseflies on it. When Jane and I finished, we woke Georgia up and she had those dead flies in her hair and on her face and clothes; hence Jane named her, "Georgia, the Queen of the Dead Flies." Jane also told me later after leaving Georgia's wake, she returned to Kismet on Fire Island where she was staying for a week, and walked past the bar as a live band was playing, "Hey Baby." She said it gave her goose bumps.

Months later and I still had trouble informing people I hadn't seen for a while who were unaware of Georgia's passing. I couldn't speak the words and I choked up. I always kept a remembrance card with me to show them as they were shocked upon learning about it. Those people that were aware but I hadn't seen, offered their sincere condolences as they expressed how shocked they were upon hearing about it. If on the phone with salespeople or reps from companies who didn't know, it was difficult saying the words, "she's gone," or "she passed away." Since 1983, I've had a remembrance card, the size of a business card with a picture of Millie on it in my wallet. Georgia commented several times for many years after our marriage, how that was the only photo I had in my wallet. She then suggested I at least carry a photo of her dog, Pookie, which I did. Then later, I also carried a wedding picture of the two of us, which I still have today. Unfortunately, I now carry her remembrance card, too.

Everyone has been very supportive during all these months following her wake, inviting me to many events to keep me busy. Neighbors on both sides of me; Sue, Jenna, Jane, Tre, Brad, and Linda had me over several times for dinner and stocked my refrigerator with ready cooked meals. I also kept myself busy doing some minor work on my house, and preparing for my move back down to the Keys for the winter. Even neighbors down there, Mark and Samantha, took care of me by opening up the house and airing it out before my arrival, having me over for dinner, and also making meals for me after I arrived. Jim and Beata, my neighbors across the canal helped also by giving me some freshly caught sea bass. But I was looking forward to some alone time so I could write about Georgia. People kept telling me to remember all the good times to help ease the pain. When I first started, I thought it would be difficult, but the process of writing down the memories of all those good times and fun we shared has eased the pain. Unfortunately, the memories of her hospital stay are still too vivid, and I'll be glad to finish this so I can release the rest of those tears I kept suppressing while writing about those bad days.

## MEMORIAL EVENT

On January twenty-fourth, her birthday and a self-proclaimed national holiday, we held a memorial for Georgia here at our house in the Keys for the people who couldn't make it up north for her wake. The flier was entitled "Memorial Event" rather than "Service," because we were not religious or church goers. She had mentioned in previous years though, that if she were to join a church, St. Peter's Catholic Church on Big Pine Key would have been a strong contender because at its St. Patrick's Day party—the only event that we attended at the church—they served Chivas Regal. After the time, date, and address, the flier simply stated, "A toast to celebrate the good times we had with Georgia. If you're up to it, write a sentence, a paragraph, or pages sharing your feelings or memories of Georgia."

## CHILDHOOD MEMORIES

Following are some of those memories of Georgia. This first one is from Mary, a childhood friend:

> *Georgia and I began our friendship in grade school and we had many terrific years together since. We grew old together. Georgia was generous to a fault in every way. She gave of herself, her time and her heart.*
>
> *I remember the day we decided to have our first drink in a bar (we were 18 years old). We went (very nervously)*

*into a place in the West Village. There were two girls sitting on one side and a couple of guys on the other side of the bar. We sat next to the girls, as we felt much safer with them. We ordered two Brandy Alexanders and one of the girls turned to the other and said, "Sweets for the sweet." Georgia and I looked at each other not fully comprehending the full meaning of what was said, but we knew instinctively to move our seats. We went over to sit where the guys were. Years later she and I laughed at this and how innocent we were.*

*Georgia had a taste for Turkish coffee, so we would go to a coffee house I believe the name was "Finjons" I would tell her that she was drinking mud with oil slick. She would laugh and drink it down. We were very happy traipsing around in the Village. She loved the art show once a year and Washington Square Park. It was very different from the Lower East Side. People were freer, they seemed to be without a care and we enjoyed it immensely.*

*My first memory of her was when we were going to a CYO dance in St. James Hall. My father did not want me to go,* so Georgia took it upon herself to try and talk him into letting me go. She was very persuasive; the upshot was that I went. I was afraid to ask, but I often wondered what she said to him to convince him. Needless to say we had a marvelous time and I believe that it was at the dance that she met Renny (her first love). We must have been about fifteen years old or so. We went to many dances and parties throughout the years. We had great friends that hung around with us on the project grounds when we were younger. We laughed, talked, and listened to our transistor radios.

Eleanor, her mother, allowed my boyfriend at the time, to give me a sixteenth birthday party in her apartment. It was terrific, Georgia put "soft shoe shuffle sand" all over the living room floor and we danced and slid to the greatest rock 'n' roll hits of the day. Years later my younger sister Raine told me that Georgia was so cool. It was such a great party and it was all Georgia's doing.

So many great memories come to me. We took off together for the World's Fair;

*we were still in high school. We ran into a group of foreigners and had a very nice experience talking with them. Georgia attracted everyone with her sweet personality and her friendly way. She was not shy and people just gravitated to her.*

*I always, in later years, admired her business attributes. When she first bought the restaurant she was in a quandary as to what to do about certain aspects of the place. She asked my opinion on one and it was a good thing she did not take my suggestion. I wanted her to put doors on the cabinets in the kitchen. How impractical that would have been. She was born with good business sense as evidenced by her successful career. She was tireless, I wrote a short speech about her for college (I went late in life). I opened with, "I have a great friend Georgia who works twenty-five hours a day." She never stopped working nor did she ever stop enjoying life. She made the most of everything, even the sad times.*

*Georgia was fiercely devoted to her mom, dad, sister, niece, and nephews. She would do anything for them. She also had the same devotion to her numerous friends. Of course the love of her life was Joe. She always spoke so highly of him to me. They were a wonderful well-matched couple.*

*I miss Georgia very much, as we all do. She died so young, as she had a lot more living to do. The world is a lot less joyous without my Georgia Girl and so are we all.*

Thank you Mary.

This next testimonial is from Donna, her "monkey" sister. She titled it,

### "What was it about this woman?"

*I met Georgia in the spring. The moment she welcomed me into her home I knew she was very special. Over the years she taught me so many things. Our lives were very opposite. She had so many friends and was the most open and loving person I have ever known. We shared so much together and spoke to each other like sisters. She always referred to me as her "Little Sister."*

*It was no accident, our meeting. A year prior, my husband and I were in the Keys. We would bring our motor home*

*down every year to camp for a couple of weeks. We never explored Big Pine but we were looking at properties. We had been visiting the Keys since the early 90's. We were driving around and found a little yellow house for sale and fell in love with the area. I always wanted a yellow house; don't ask me why. Well, while making a decision on the way back to NY the owner called and said he had a cash buyer. I was devastated. Anyway, what I'm trying to get at is that the day I met Georgia at her home in Big Pine we went out on her screened deck overlooking the canal. I looked across the canal and there was the little yellow house we were so interested in buying.*

*When I told her the story we both thought it was such a crazy coincidence! It wasn't. My Dad worked for Georgia many years ago and he felt compelled to see her again and see how she was doing after all these years. We had no idea she was in Florida. It was meant to be that she came into my life. She was my fishing buddy, my shoulder when I needed her. She was there for me no matter what. She gave her whole self to me. I loved her; our time with our "Monkeys" was kinda weird to some, but to us, it was Magical! I miss her face, her smile, her bitching, her laugh. I know I will never know anyone quite like her again in my lifetime. We used to talk for hours on the phone and at the end of each conversation before our goodbye she would say, "I love you baby," and I would say, "I love you." Then she would say, "I love you more!" KALINEÉHTA (Greek for good night) my love, I will have you in my heart forever. HAPPY BIRTHDAY in heaven. I'm sure it's a national holiday up there too! I LOVE YOU MORE!*

Thank you, Donna.

## MONKEY ABUSE

BetteAnn had this to say about Georgia:

*We met Georgia about twelve years ago when Georgia told our friend Gene to invite us to one of her dinner parties. We were complete strangers, but Georgia welcomed us into her home and life with open arms, as she did with everyone she met. That was just the beginning of a very special friendship I had with Georgia that would continue and become close even after the passing of Gene. Throughout the years our friendship became more like "sisters" as we laughed together, cried together, and shared many conversations just like sisters. It always made me feel so good when she would hold my hand and look me in the eyes and tell me, "I love you BetteAnn." She always made me feel like one of her special friends and I knew she loved me unconditionally, just as I loved her unconditionally. Georgia had a heart of gold, and was one of the most generous and loving people I will ever know.*

BetteAnn continues:

*Here are some of the special memories we will hold in our hearts forever; of course I will always think of her as the "Monkey Lady" and all the pleasure she had collecting all of her "babies." Her monkeys always brought out the child in her and I loved her childlike voice when she talked to her monkeys or spoke of them.*

*Our birthdays are about six months apart, and Georgia always loved to tease* and remind me that I was older than her. She would always say I was her older sister, and I would say, "Well, that makes me the wiser sister." One of the best memories I will remember, about her birthday, was the smile and excitement on her face when I would make her a Monkey Cake. I will never forget her smile from cheek to cheek, and her joy and excitement when I surprised her with that first monkey cake. That excitement continued with the second and third monkey cakes. I enjoyed making them for her because she would get so excited at receiving them and she knew I thought she was a very special lady. She never failed to show me just how much she loved them and appreciated the time and love I put into making them.

When you guys would leave for NY for the summer, Georgia would always ask me to "babysit" one or two of her special monkeys. Knowing how much she loved her monkeys and how much they were a part of her, (and that she would also miss them) I decided to have some fun with her and take pictures of "Sock," (one of the monkeys left in my care) doing *various things and send the pictures to her with a note from Sock. I think the one she enjoyed the most was when I took Sock to the rental with me and had him help me clean the toilets and writing his "mommy" to tell her that Bette was making him clean toilets and that didn't make him happy and he missed her. I laughed so hard doing this, but I don't think as hard as Georgia laughed seeing the pictures and the big kick she got out of it. One of my favorite memories of Georgia will always be of how cute and childlike she would get over her monkeys. She taught me that we were never too old to be silly and have fun.*

*The greatest memories we will never forget will be of sharing the laughter, great stories, and fun we had at the many social dinner parties and holidays at your home, not to forget the great food and drinks. You both graciously included us in your circle of friends. Those were the best of times, and we will forever miss those times.*

*The Polish party and the making of the homemade sauerkraut and Polish sausage. Also, you both always made our friends and neighbors feel welcome by including them in the fun and great Polish food. Many times on our way out the door after a gathering, Georgia would turn on the jukebox as we danced and sang while she threw pennies up in the air as "Pennies from Heaven" played. It was always a great way to say goodnight!*

*It was always cute to watch Georgia talk Ski into singing "Georgia On My Mind" to her. She always made him feel like he was a great singer even though he didn't think he could sing. But he enjoyed pleasing her and making her happy, so he did. We will never be able to hear that song without thinking of her.*

*Oh, and that cheesecake! No one will ever make a cheesecake as good as hers. Even though it was a lot of work, she made it for all of us so often and with so much love knowing how much everyone enjoyed it. She was so sweet when she made sure to cut and wrap a large piece and hide it in the refrigerator for Ski to take home before everyone ate it all. She always made him feel so special, and he loved every bite of it. I sure hope I can make her recipe for him at least half as good as she did. I know with every bite, he will think of her and how special she was, and how special she made him feel.*

*The fun we had going to garage sales until I stopped going because I didn't need any more "junk." It was always so much fun to find that special treasure real cheap! The not so funny time (yes it was funny) we stopped at a yard sale and the lady had cactus pieces at the end of the driveway for anyone to take. As I went to open the back window of the truck so Georgia could put the big piece in, she wasn't paying any attention when I stopped walking and she ran that cactus piece right into my butt leaving thorns that Ski spent the rest of the day pulling out. Not to mention how hard it was to sit and drive home that day with thorns in my butt! Still makes me laugh to this day!*

*I told Georgia the story of the Pennies from Heaven. As you know, the story was that finding a penny on the ground was supposed to be from people we loved that had passed on, and that meant they were letting us know they were thinking of us and watching over us. From then on, she would pick up every penny she found and give it to me insisting it was from Gene. Well a few days after Georgia's passing, I found two pennies together on the ground. I picked the pennies up with tears in my eyes and told Ski that I knew it was a sign from Georgia and Gene and that they were together and this was their way of telling me. I said out loud, "Gene please take care of my dear friend Georgia!" I know in my heart they are together looking down at us and watching over us.*

*Joe, you were the love of Georgia's life. She loved you so much. She talked to me often about how happy she was that you two had a second chance. You could always see the twinkle in her eyes when she mentioned your name or would say Joe in her childlike voice. I'll always remember her excitement of your second wedding and of her knowing that meant she would spend the rest of her life with you. We were so happy that we could share in your happiness and love for each other that day.*

*This has been a very difficult six*

*months for me with the loss of my dear girlfriend Georgia, and my life will never be the same without her. Georgia had a very generous and kind heart, making friends easily and including them in her circle of friends, as she did with me. She was quick to also include many of my friends in her circle. I'm so happy that I have so many precious memories of her and so happy for the time that she was in my life. She was loved by everyone she met. I will miss all the laughs, tears, and fun times we shared. But most of all, I will miss her. It's so hard to lose the special people we love, and it leaves such a void in my life without her. "I Love you Georgia."*

Thank you BetteAnn, how true, for all of us.

The following note is from Ron, and then a testimonial from his wife, Mary; both had always invited us to their home for Thanksgiving.

*Georgia—Memories of her coming by our house on Saturday mornings—bragging about the yard sales she had been to— excited to show off her purchases. Having her over to dinner at our house once when we were having ribs. She ate some—asked how I cooked them and said they were good. Then she told me when she used to cook ribs, people lined up around the block to get some. Memories of how excited she would get about the Polish party—even called me the "Pierogi King." We enjoyed Georgia. She came to Thanksgiving at the house for many years—always said it's great to not have to cook—and then she would smile.—we remember.*

Thank you Ron.

## "SALE-ING" HINTS

The next testimonial is from Mary:

### My Friend Georgia

*A cook*

*An entertainer*

*A friend with strong opinions*

*A bargain hunter*

*A lady rescuer of boaters*

*A collector of:*

    *Monkeys*

    *Knick knacks*

    *Of people's hearts*

As a bargain hunter, there was no better. If ever one had the opportunity to start an early Saturday morning adventure out onto U.S. 1, zigzagging thru traffic, following newspaper ads and road signs…the driver getting the navigational rights and lefts from Georgia, sitting in the shotgun position, then you truly have lived thru a thrill ride. Upon successful arrival at the "roadside bargain center" the real fun started. The shopping list was rechecked (yes, there was an actual written list).

Georgia would target the coveted item and the offering would begin…it was like an auction in reverse…price started high and she would bid down…99% of the time she was successful in her quest. On the rare occasion when she walked away empty handed the 1% disappointment left plenty of "conversation material" while we continued our path to the next unsuspecting victim!

On occasion there would be a special find, not on the coveted list. It would be something she knew we had to have. She would make sure they made their way to *our downstairs "gathering area." I have a few of these items, a glance in their direction always brings a little smile and a memory, knowing she "hit the nail on the head" with that find.*

*What grown woman buys tickets to a Broadway show written and produced to attract and entertain children...Georgia loved monkeys and Curious George was a monkey with a story line of mischief, mistakes, correction and forgiveness... all set to music and presented on the big stage...Georgia would hijack a child, with parental permission and the two would take in the lights and sounds of New York's show district...Georgia always seemed to recall the event with more excitement and enthusiasm than her much younger accomplice.*

*All are things I remember, to each a story can be told, but my favorite would have to be Georgia's unusual affinity for collecting MONKEYS...I often told her the plush, stuffed, sometimes worn and tired variety only stood in for the "real life personalities" she collected and invited into her life...a cast of characters with accents from Texas drawls, Southern twang, Louisiana coonass, and it goes without saying, heavy New Yorker's lingo. Noteworthy: We shared her first drink from Social Security check at the Tiki Bar...remember that day Sam?*

*Georgia's famous cheesecake stories and love of them will be shared by Betty and Ski...*

*Georgia's pride and joy, the love of her life, Joe, was always a topic of conversation that brought a round of new stories, of a romantic Joe, through pictures and stories I got a glimpse of the "soft side" of Georgia—a real treasure in any gal relationship.*

*Be mindful as I write this, I also recall being told and I quote "to shut the F_ _ _ up and leave me alone...."*

*What more can I add...volumes, but some things need to stay tucked away in the quiet part of my memory.*

Thank you, Mary.

This next one is from Linda, who helped pack the monkeys and also flew up north for Georgia's wake.

### "GEORGIA ON MY MIND"

*Georgia taught me everything I know about yard sales. As you all know, she loved a yard sale and did not like driving, so sometimes I would be her "Driving Miss Georgia."*

*Lesson:*

*1. Drive by real slow to see if it was even worth stopping*

*2. Don't hover over an item*

*3. Always have a pocket full of quarters*

*4. She'd get mad at me if I paid full price*

*5. She would make her offer, hand them the money and walk away, and they took it! She loved the hunt and the haggle.*

*The most important thing I learned from Georgia was that LOVE had no boundaries at her table. Georgia was the most generous person I ever met. There was always enough food for another plate and if there was not enough room for another chair she would put up another table and move there. Everyone felt her love. My mom and sister were invited; everyone was invited.*

*I have a plaque that hangs above my door that says, "Live well, Love much,*

*Laugh often,"* *which exemplifies her well.*
*Which, of course, Georgia bought for me*
*at a yard sale.*

    *Like no other I have ever known*
    *How fondly of Georgia I had grown*
    *Georgia has the heart of gold for*
    *Everyone she loved and everyone she*
*told.*

    *Her Friends were family and her*
*family were friends.*

    *GOD GOT A GOOD ONE, now she's*
*laughing and singing with Aunt Mary and*
*Uncle John. Happy Birthday Georgia.*

Thank you, Linda.

Here's a note from Steve and Sharon:

*Dear Georgia, When I first met you in*
*2008 we were never introduced as you*
*left my yard sale on Buttonwood without*
*telling me your name. Quite frankly it*
*did not matter at that time. You had*
*purchased/stolen a red wagon from me*
*for approximately three dollars. My*
*asking price was TWELVE dollars. You*
*were so nice, the way you haggled me*
*down, I was laughing inside. The way*

*you said, "Honey, look I'll give you three dollars cash, OK?" You were so nice about it I just could not say no. When you left, I said to my wife, Sharon, whoever that woman was, she really is something else! About a year and a half later, our mutual friend, Trish, invited us to her house for a Greek cheese cook-off with you and Joe, and lots of laughs were had. "Opa."*

*Then sometime later on after a day of yard sales, you and Trish stopped by our house on Buttonwood. The first thing you said to me was, "Honey, I think I've been here before, did you ever have a yard sale?" I said to you, "Honey, you're the one who beat me up on the red wagon." Well, we laughed and laughed.*

*Then you invited us to your Pierogi party and we got to know Joe better and all of your wonderful friends. Every one of your parties were great! They were very special to us. We really liked the time, energy, originality, fun, and especially the food and the cooking together that went into your and Joe's parties.*

*We can't talk about all the good times we had, but I did want to tell you that you*

*really touched Mary, at Joma's restaurant
when you guys came up to the Catskills.
What a fun night! She knew right away
you were a good person, as we all did. Red
Solo Cup, I lift you up, proceed to party!
Thank you Georgia.*

> *All our love, Steve and Sharon*
> *AKA The Round House People*

The following was received via email a little while after the memorial:

*When a person makes an impression
on others that will always remain with
them, they are a very special person!
Georgia was one of those people. Georgia's
love of others and her bubbly, friendly,
personality made her an instant friend
to all, especially to us. Georgia made the
"best" cheesecake ever, and she was kind
enough to share her recipe with us. We
will always remember her every time we
enjoy a piece of the magic her famous
cheesecake has. Georgia will live on in
the hearts and minds of those she touched
while she was here with us.*

> *Ron & Barb (neighbors of Bette & Ski)*

And Mark contributed the following:

### *"Where is the bride?"*

*Georgia was married 3 times in her life, in her 20's to Joe I, in her 40's to Joe II, and in her 50's to Joe III, the "Redo."*

*I don't know the exact dates and ages for the 3 but I do know that Georgia and Joe were on a "break" for about 5 years until they remarried 1/22/2005 in Key Colony Beach, Florida. I was in charge of walking the bride down the aisle and giving her away. It was an outdoor ceremony at their home by the pool. Georgia and I were stationed on the side of the house by the AC condenser. We were supposed to walk around to the pool when "Here Comes the Bride" started to play.*

*Well, you can't have a wedding without toasts so as we waited to hear the music we started toasting with a bottle of Chivas and 2 shot glasses we had with us! We were laughing and shooting and swapping funny memories. The AC was continuously running and we never heard the song. After 4 shots and 5 music intros someone ran around the corner and said, "Come on guys the*

*music has played 5 times!" My only duty
that day and we both missed the cue for
me to walk her "down the aisle" to give
her away. Well, it gave us something to
laugh about when reminiscing about
the wedding, but they lived happily ever
after, after the second time.*

Thanks Mark.

## TRAIN TO MANHATTAN

The following was submitted by Samantha via email:

***Stories of Georgia….***
*Lord, I met Georgia and Joe in 2007 and
was welcomed with open arms and felt as
if I had just met the parents I NEVER had.*

***"Sleepy's"***
*On our trips to NY to visit Joe & Georgia,
at least one day out of the trip was spent
taking the train into Manhattan to visit
selected "tourist" sites, like the Intrepid,
Statue of Liberty, Ellis Island, Hell's
Kitchen, Battery Park etc., plus every bar
that was open in our path. To pass the time*

on the train ride I noticed a store named "Sleepy's" was showing up a lot! A bar on every corner and a Sleepy's in the middle of the block. We came up with the idea to have a game to see who could be the first to spot one while on that train with the winner not having to pay for their lunch. We even took Maimou into a local Sleepy's on another day to have his picture taken on one of their mattresses!

A little side story when visiting the Intrepid—it being a government facility there were metal detectors to walk through. That year one of Georgia's customary flasks was a fake cell phone which she gave to Mark to carry for her. Mark pulled 2 "cell phones" out of his pockets, and put them both through the metal detector as the guard held his mixed drink for him to walk through the detector! NEVER a dull moment!

### "Slice of Bread"

Georgia was always watching her weight and she was very creative in how she counted her calories. I never had any idea that the calories in a slice of white bread *was the same as a Bud Light; well it is! So that was our code, "Honey - do you have a slice of bread!" Didn't matter the time of day, the bread was always available.*

### "Garage Sales"

*One of her passions was garage sales, she could never pass one up. She took me under her wing, explained the process and let me tag along and watch the master! How many Saturday's we got in the Jeep, stopped for coffee and sometimes an oatmeal cookie and traveled through the lower Keys hunting bargains.*

*I've watched her walk in, survey the products, pick out what she wanted, approach the owner and either wear them down to her price or place a couple of dollars, and sometimes just quarters, in their hand and just keep walking. People were usually so stunned by this process she was in the car with the door shut before they ever realized what happened!*

### "Capful of Scotch"

*On one of the trips Mark and I made to NY in September, we made our usual one* day train trip into Manhattan. On these yearly train trips Georgia always made sure there was a flask or two of Chivas Regal in her purse and someone's pocket.

That night on our return trip back to Lindenhurst, as Georgia and Mark were drinking out of their flasks, this gentleman across the aisle was salivating over their flasks. He was returning from the city after visiting his ailing mother. Georgia's predicament, having never met a stranger, was she wanted to share but didn't want a stranger to drink from her flask and had no cups when he mentioned he could use a drink. She decided she would feed him capfuls of Chivas from her flask! Problem Solved! We never mentioned to Georgia that the same top that touched the stranger's lips was now capping her flasks!

### "Wet Willy"
Georgia was a very popular young woman which lasted until the day she died. The one story of "another man" that stands out in my mind was a gentleman that visited the bar her mother worked in when Georgia

was in her 20's. This "gentleman" was notorious for giving people "wet willies" (a wet finger in the ear) and Georgia hated this. Well, one day this guy made the mistake of catching Georgia and giving her a wet willy. She was very upset and later complained to some of the "family" bar patrons. Georgia said she never saw that guy, ever, again.

### "Train shut down"

One year we had an issue with a lake house repair and Mark had to stay behind in Eatonton and I went to NY by myself. So Georgia and I went into Manhattan, just the 2 of us. One of her bucket list items was to walk the Brooklyn Bridge so we did! We stayed in town all day, ate well and then went to Penn Station to catch a train back home. Well at the stop just before ours our train conked out! We had to leave the station, find a place to call Joe and wait for him to drive 35 miles to pick us up. Well as in most cases we decided to wait in a neighborhood bar! Low and behold the bartender had worked for Georgia in her German restaurant and *she called in 2 other past employees! Seems like everywhere we went, a past employee came out of the woodwork.*

*The one constant knowing Georgia and Joe is realizing how much they loved each other and would do anything for each other. She cooked, he ate, she watched. She gardened, he watched, he bragged on her (she could make anything grow!) Mark and I got to be in charge of putting in the surprise autopilot in Joe's boat while they vacationed in Mexico. He was surprised and happy to receive that gift even though, she told me later, it was more for her benefit because it made it easier for her if it were just the two of them trolling as she had to pull in the other lines, maintain course, fluctuate speed and be ready with a gaff while he was reeling in the big catch.*

*Turnabout—Joe got even when, at his request, we coordinated the installation of a new washer and dryer for a surprise Christmas present for her when they again were in Mexico. Even with her tiny feet, the shoes to fill for Georgia are enormous!*

*Love you and miss you!*

*Mark, Samantha and your dog, Layla!*

Thank you Samantha.

Stephen remembers:

### *"The Best Boss I Never Had."*

*So in Jan. of '86 while I was still commuting from Astoria to Lindenhurst we had a very bad snow storm. Trains were delayed or cancelled so my boss Georgia suggested that I stay over rather than try to get home and back for work the following morning. At the tender age of 22 I wasn't exactly sure how to respond but Georgia told me not to worry—she had a king size bed and anyway she "wasn't gonna bite me."*

*I accepted her generous offer and we had a few drinks before retiring to Georgia's upstairs apartment. True to her word—she didn't bite me and even had a freshly laundered shirt for me to wear for my next shift in the morning.*

*Breakfast was made and consumed and I went to work. Georgia was busy that morning and didn't spend much time in the bar until mid lunch. We would have a full bar every day from the local Nynex workers grabbing a quick wurst sandwich and a drink, and this day was no exception... So when we had a full bar (and Georgia had a full audience) she came downstairs, made sure everyone was watching, and then swung my shirt from the previous day around her head telling me, "Ya forgot your shirt last night hon!"*

*Everyone at the bar and probably the dining room) loved it—I was complimented on being such a quick mover and asked if I was going to change the restaurant from German to Irish and planning to move in full time.... I was as red as the German tie she made me wear, but I probably made an extra twenty at the bar that day—like I said—Georgia was the best boss I never had...*

*Stephen*

Thank you, Stephen.

Carol says,

*Joe, as far as a remembrance, there are so many shared memories that I am lucky to have. Here is one:*

*Georgia was so kind to my father that she easily became a part of our family. One weekend, she and Joe joined us on a* camping trip. Enjoying the campfire one evening, we began to talk about my dad. I said that he was getting old and I wanted to get to go to Germany with him as Georgia had done, so he could show me where he lived and meet some of the relatives still living in Germany. Georgia said, "So what are we waiting for—let's go."

Well my husband Chet and I have two sons and things just don't seem to happen that easily. Georgia saw my father at the Restaurant and said, "Onkel, why don't we go to Germany and you pay for each of your children to go?" That was all the prodding he needed! He paid airfare for all five of his children. Some of us went alone, others brought a spouse, and I was able to have my husband and two sons come along.

It was a dream come true for me. We saw the home where he grew up, his town, his church, the spot where his tongue really did get stuck to a metal pole, we swam in the town pool, and met many relatives. My sons' lives were enriched. Besides our family, Mike and Peggy and their daughter Jessica and her friend joined us, as well *as Franky and Kiki, our brother-in-law's brother and wife, and Connie.*

*Our group totaled twenty people traveling throughout Germany in five separate cars. This was all because Georgia said, "Why not—let's go—why wait!" She was a doer, making things happen for those around her, giving of herself. It was a blast!!!*

*Love, Carol*

Thank You, Carol.

And Dale remembers this,

*I have had hundreds of adventures with Georgia but there is one in particular that stands out. Georgia and I were down in the Florida Keys attending a fishing trip with John and Chris Davis. It was a Saturday afternoon when John received a phone call, which informed him he had to fly home by Sunday for his Grandson's Communion. Georgia, myself, John, and Chris got into John's beige Lincoln Town Car and headed to the Key West airport. I had just bought a brand new bathing suit and left it in the backseat when the four of us went in to buy our tickets.*

*After we got our tickets we headed*

back to the car. John and Chris sat in the front seat, and Georgia and I sat in the backseat. Georgia turned to me and said, "Where is the bag with your new bathing suit; it isn't in the car?" Thinking I forgot it in the airport, we all went inside to try and find it. We looked for a few minutes and couldn't find it so we all headed back to the car again. Again, John and Chris took the front seat, and Georgia and I took the backseat. We were all dumbfounded that someone would steal a bathing suit.

Just then, Georgia noticed cigarette butts in the ashtray. Since none of us were smokers we were confused as to how these butts got into the ashtray. Georgia looked out the windows and noticed a Lincoln identical to ours, three parking spots over. We all got out of the car, and walked over to the other Lincoln. Low and behold there was my bathing suit in the backseat of our car. Not once, but twice we all got into the wrong car all together. We laughed for an hour before we could drive away.

Thank you Dale.

And Debbie remembers her sister,

*My Dear Georgia. My Big Sister of three. That is what she called us, and that is what she was to me. Met Georgia in the early stages of her restaurant career. She was an interesting woman, she worked like a dog and partied like there was no tomorrow.*

*Georgia took on employees as friends and family that needed a helping hand at life, and that's where I came in. During the eight years I worked for her she taught me responsibility, self-esteem, and respect for the elderly (who were a big part of her life, including my mother, Marge). She always told me to put away a part of my income and save it. One day I would thank her for it. She made me a better person/waitress.*

*Georgia always wanted to have a party and that is what she did. Every Saturday night "Sandbar Mike" and the boys came on down to the restaurant and made music; at least that's what they called it. We danced and sang and drank. Sandbar Mike also conducted Georgia's annual fishing trip. She was an avid fisherwoman. She also turned an ordinary Atlantic City bus trip into an unforgettable time. The bus ride was the highlight, just being altogether. She also had an annual German Festival and a Greek Night having everyone who attended become honorary Germans or Greeks for each event.*

*When I was eight months pregnant with my son Patrick, Georgia had a pool to see who could guess the baby's height and weight. Everyone was a winner just being in Georgia's life. Luckily Patrick had a chance to be a part of her life also.*

*Whatever hobbies Georgia took on, she did them to the fullest, teaching me most of her secrets. Gardening, cooking, canning, and chocolate making were some of her favorite ones. She took pride in teaching those who wanted to learn. And once again she made a party out of her parties.*

*WE LOVE SUSHI. Georgia, Dale, and I (the three sisters) went almost every week while she was on Long Island. Kotobuki was our favorite place for sushi and then we would go next door to Pace's. One of my favorite times there was on her birthday. My friend was at her best.*

*I bought her a gift including a miniskirt and thigh-high stockings. Thinking that nobody could see her, Georgia changed her clothes behind the piano not knowing there was a mirror above her. We could not stop laughing. Lol. She looked hot.*

*Years have passed and our friendship has grown along with our bucket list. We have traveled from East to West, vacationing in Montauk, fishing on the "Lazybones," and riding in a limo to New York City to see a play or visit restaurants. She obtained a book on the best bars and restaurants in NYC. So what she wanted to accomplish was to go to every one of them and have her book signed. We put in a lot of miles in a lot of days.*

*We were sisters for thirty-five years. I just hope that I've grown to be as much of a role model as she was to me.*

*I LOVE YOU GEORGIA and*
*MISS YOU EVERYDAY*
*Your sister, DEBBIE*

Thank You, Debbie.

*Her "Baby"*

*Celebrating Greek Night*

*Her Stein Sign*

*Paddling down the Peconic River*

*The Three Sisters (Georgia, Debbie & Dale)*

# EPILOGUE

Some of these separate events I've written about might not be in chronological order. With all that we have done in our lives, it's hard to remember the sequence of events, with some just being a vague recollection. When meeting someone we hadn't seen for a while, they would ask, "Do you remember such and such an event." Most of the time I do remember the event, but there are times the details are a blur.

Georgia believed her greatest achievement was the establishment and running of Georgia's German Restaurant. While it was a major milestone, it was not her greatest. Her greatest achievement was the group of friendships she accumulated during her lifetime. Friends of ours, John and Millie, gave out tee-shirts at one of their barbeques that read, "Friends are life's most valuable assets," thus defining Georgia as very rich. As you can see, a story about Georgia is a story about other people. These friends enriched her life as much as she enriched theirs.

There is anger, sorrow, and emptiness in her passing—anger at "the powers that be" for taking her away, sorrow that we will no longer have the fun we once enjoyed, and the emptiness of knowing she's not around anymore. Months later, the finality of it hit me like a board striking me across the chest taking my breath away. When it first happened, I knew she was gone, but months later, it still hurt.

Now a year later, the tears start flowing when I think about those last three hospital days, or when I look at her empty chair and realize she will no longer be sitting there; the finality is realized. It hurts. That's it. She's gone. It's then that I have to remind myself of the good times we had together and remember during her lifetime, "No One Had More Fun" than Georgia. But I wish she wasn't right. Damn it.

*A Toast to All; Thank You.*

# ABOUT THE AUTHOR

**JOE MCKASTY** is a Long Island native who was raised in Lindenhurst, dropped out of high school on his sixteenth birthday, and at twenty joined the Army's 101st Airborne Division for three years. He worked as a carpenter for seventeen years and then as a special education vocational teacher for twenty-five years. Being a slow learner, he didn't get his B.S. degree until the year he retired. He is a sun-bird spending the summers on Long Island and the winters down in the Keys.

His first marriage to Nancy produced two sons, Michael and Joseph. His second common-law marriage to Millie produced four stepdaughters, Georgia, Linda, Donna, and Kelly. He was married twice to Georgia, producing a multitude of new friends and barrels of monkeys. He is grateful for the fun times he has spent with each of them.

# No One
# Had More
# FUN

For more information regarding
Joe McKasty and his work,
Email Joe at joe@noonehadmorefun.com

This book is also available as an eBook.
Additional print copies and eBook downloads
may be purchased online from:
www.LegworkTeam.com; www.Amazon.com;
or www.BarnesandNoble.com

You can also obtain a copy of the book by
ordering it from your favorite bookstore.

CPSIA information can be obtained at www.ICGtesting.com
Printed in the USA
BVOW11s1117040116

431702BV00010B/29/P